# The Call of the Dervish

PIR VILAYAT INAYAT KHAN

# The Call of the Dervish

by

Pir Vilayat Inayat Khan

OMEGA PUBLICATIONS

New Lebanon

## ACKNOWLEDGEMENTS

The author would like to express his gratitude to Sajjada Kopelman, who carried out the demanding task of selecting the lectures that make up this book from among the very large number of transcripts that touch upon the topics covered here, and to Alison Kilgour, who translated the spoken word into writing with perception and sensitivity.

Cover art drawn by Jeannette Gawry Micoleau.
The cover design was conceived by Abi'l Khayr and executed by Barkat Curtin/Spring Hill Graphics.

OMEGA PUBLICATIONS
RD 1 BOX 1030E
New Lebanon, NY 12125-9801

ISBN 0 930872-44-4
10 9 8 7 6 5 4 3 2

# CONTENTS

# The Veil of the Beloved

For there to be a change from the lonely state of delusion—if we are really to fulfill our purpose in life—we have to go about it in a very strong way. We have to plug in to something so enormously great that we can't say we grasp it, but rather that we are grasped by it. Our minds tell us that it is the divine splendor, but all our ideas and representations fall by the way and seem so futile, and what we do to bring about the change we seek seems to be so very inadequate.

Perhaps we are shaken to our foundations when we do spiritual practices, and it seems like a big deal until we realize that it is just a pinprick in the whole process of life; but sometimes things happen that cause us to be transported. Something is suddenly triggered off, or it seems as if we have lost our precarious foothold on the world. Sometimes it's so strong that our foundations are made to quake by the power that is coming through.

This is because the world as we thought we knew it is such a very small, fragmentary expression of reality. It's like a ripple on the ocean of reality, and at no time can we ever expect to grasp all the greatness of reality, which is the greatness of God. And yet it seems that the objective is the homonization of God—that He should become a being with a body through us. This is the making of the king.

We have to reach beyond the world so that God may become a reality in us. It may seem terribly presumptuous to say that, since only in the *rasul*, the prophet, can the divine Being reach fulfillment; but we are, perhaps, sketches in the preparation of various works of art—the trials and errors that must be made so that one day there may be a masterpiece. However fragmentary it may be, when the being of God comes through, we are overwhelmed with delight. It's like a sign from the One we love that there is indeed a little bit of reciprocation after so much abandonment ensuing from our alienation. Of course, we can only manifest God inasmuch as we know God, and we can only know God inasmuch as we know Him in ourselves. We discover Him in ourselves: that is our passive response to His action in us. Still, this response seems so very small and inadequate: what do we know of Him that we may manifest Him? What we know of the universe is so little, and the whole universe is so little in comparison with the divine perfection. How can we claim to manifest the divine perfection?

When we are prepared to make an effort to depart from our usual alienation and have the courage to go through the dark night, when there seem to be no results from our efforts and we have to cope with the abyss of our personal selves and struggle with despair because we are not reaching beyond— even when we are tested in the extremes of abandonment—at the moment when everything seems to be useless and lost, there is sometimes a tiny indication—*ayat* as the Sufis say—a sign, or perhaps a symbol, as if we were able to perceive the signal of a being in outer space who is beckoning us to believe in his presence: a silent voice that we suddenly plug into. This is just a metaphor, of course; we might say that what happens to us is that we are suddenly catapulted while we are trying in vain to lift our consciousness, when all the thoughts of the world in all their sham come back because of the conditioning of the mind. We go on struggling, and suddenly it's as if something were unleashed, and we are catapulted into what seem like other spheres. It's as if there were several universes, one within the other, or in totally different space-time relationships—we don't know.

There is no element of comparison: what we find is totally different from what we thought. As a matter of fact, our representations, including the attempts at description I have made here, are not only totally inadequate, but may stand in the way of our experience. We have to be prepared to find that it is totally different from anything we have ever thought. For instance, we may hope to reach upwards into other universes, and it may turn out to be the other way around: something of the nature of the modes of the being of God may begin to make itself manifest in our being; and our receptivity or capacity to let it come through is our response to what is coming through.

It is only in the divine essence that all is one without any multiplicity whatsoever—which means without the deterioration, degradation, or alienation that arises from the individual will. There is a coordination behind everything, and we know that it's an unbroken wholeness, but do we know what unity means? We can only know unity when we are carried beyond our idiosyncrasies, our wills, and our individual consciousness, and stripped of all those qualities of our being that have alienated us from the divine hallmark that constitutes the essence of our being.

This is what we are doing in the spiritual path: undergoing a stripping of what the Sufis call *nazutiat*, the physical plane. Everything is included in the divine nature, but it has been alienated, degraded, deviated, limited, and fragmented, and it is suffering entropy or disorder. It's all beyond our understanding: it seems so contradictory. Is it a fulfillment of His nostalgia—*ishq*—that He should become a being in the physical world, which so alienates itself from His original purity? Then what is the meaning of the stripping into the beyond that is beyond the beyond? The mind will never be able to encompass all of this; we only know that we are groping, and sometimes guided; and when we depart from our secure foothold in our minds, we are overwhelmed with the sublime splendor that is itself a garb—the veil covering the face of the Beloved.

So from the human vantage point, even the splendor that we so glorify is a veil, and we can be so enamored of the glory that we fail to experience communion with the Being; yet what avers itself to be a veil from our point of view is from the divine point of view that with which He manifests Himself. Then we realize that by knowing Him or knowing whatever we can of Him through ourselves, we are still not reaching Him. We can only really know God by loving—and that is a very painful path, because it doesn't seem to be reciprocated: we go from abandonment to abandonment—and even through betrayal.

It seems easy at first: how could anyone not love all that is beautiful and wonderful? We soon learn that this is like loving a person for the beauty of his face, which is not loving, but admiring. The path of love is a path for the madmen who are prepared to be thwarted in this, the most sacred thing in the world. The power behind which the whole universe revolves is the power of love. We know love as liking people, as passion, as compassion; we know it in tenderness, in kindness, in admiration, in friendship, and in many other manifestations and expressions of love. But if you could ever reach love in its unadulterated, overwhelming reality, it would shatter you more surely than the most overwhelming knowledge of meaningfulness. In fact, you can only manifest the divine Being by involving yourself in the trauma of divine love, when you realize that all you thought you knew was absolutely worthless.

We cannot existentiate God by knowing Him, because our knowledge of Him is so totally puny—except for those moments when, as al-Hallaj says, God descends from His pinnacle into your heart and overwhelms you with His knowledge; and then there is no way in which you can possibly encompass it or reflect it, or in any way respond to it.

I know I'm talking nonsense here. That's the language of the Sufis: it doesn't tally with the knowledge of the world, and it cannot fit into any compartment, yet it is the ultimate realization. In comparison, any knowledge that a philosopher or scientist can cull from the nature of phenomena is as inadequate as Newton's theory in comparison with Einstein's. This is the knowledge that transforms beings, and that creates the human being whose dimensions are far vaster than one could ever know.

CHAPTER 1

# The Search for Meaning

Just imagine that you have an opportunity to ask an oracle two questions. What questions would you ask? Obviously, the first question would be, "What is the purpose of my life?" And the second of the two most pertinent of all questions is, "What is all this about? What is life all about? What is the meaning of it all?" In India, people do travel thousands of miles to consult a holy man, who is indeed supposed to be an oracle and to have all the answers; whether he is a rishi in the Himalayas, a dervish, or a Buddhist monk makes no difference.

You might expect a paradoxical answer to your questions, because our understanding is limited. As Hazrat Pir-o-Murshid Inayat Khan, the founder of the Sufi Order in the West, has said, the purpose of life is like a horizon: the further one advances, the further it recedes. As you grow in understanding, you see that beyond the purpose you were able to grasp earlier, there is a still further purpose; and, of course, there comes a time when you realize that it is not satisfying enough just to follow a purpose that seems to make sense for yourself. You can only muster all the potentialities in your being when you are serving a purpose beyond yourself. This is the great power of religion: it carries people beyond the limits of their individual selves, and you are never so much yourself as when you are carried beyond the limits of yourself. Thinking in terms of your individual self, you can't see things clearly.

The greatest thing that can happen to a human being is to become conscious of the magnificence of the meaningfulness of life. The miracle of life is that we are actually able to have access to the thinking behind the universe—or, as the Sufis say, access to the thinking of God. It's that understanding that is the great miracle of life. Of course, realization demands of you that you let go of all your basic assumptions. The history of science, for example, is fraught with assumptions abandoned one after the other—beginning with the assumption that what you perceive is right. For instance, the sun appears to revolve around the earth, but in fact it is the earth that revolves around the sun. Even the assumptions that two parallel lines never meet or that matter is solid have been disproved; and although we know that there should be discrete objects, we now find that in the holographic view there is only one reality concerning all things—which is what the Sufis have always said.

The latest thing in science is giving up logic; we are obliged, for instance, to accept that we are both particles and wavelike at the same time—in fact, we are obliged to give up all the basic assumptions of logic. This is, of course, a basic prerequisite for reaching realization. Contemplatives since the beginning of time have found that it was their minds that were standing in the way of their realization.

The particular perspective of Sufism is that our basic mistake may be that we are always thinking of ourselves as the subject that knows. According to Sufism, there is only one subject who knows, and that is God; we are, therefore, the media through which the divine self-realization takes place. Our whole grammar has to be rethought; instead of saying, "I think," as Descartes said, you have to say, "I am thought": you have to think of yourself in passive rather than active terms. Most of us are not used to that way of thinking, but it is necessary if we want to understand meaningfulness in our lives. Many people come to talk to me about their problems, but I can see that behind the cover of their superficial problems, the deepest problem is whether all of this makes sense—and if it does, how can you account for the fact that the most incongruous things happen? Is there such a thing as God behind all this, or is it just our imagination? The issue is not even any longer the issue of faith in God, but whether everything makes sense—and although it's ultimately the same thing, this is the particular point at which our minds are challenged.

Exactly as the scientists have abandoned many assumptions in order to be able to enter into the programming of the universe and to understand its meaningfulness, there are people in religious fields who have to abandon anthropomorphical concepts of God and realize that these are simply models like those used in science. These models have been helpful for people who needed something tangible to hold on to, but the sense of meaningfulness is a matter of experience, which itself has to be interpreted. Our experience shows us that the sun turns around the earth, so to arrive at the truth we have to reinterpret our experience. In fact, we are constantly interpreting experience. But there is a lack of sincerity in substituting a concept for an experience. This is what Christ meant by "vain repetition"—using the word "God" without meaning God. In our time, we feel a great need to get into experience rather than live in concepts.

Because experience has to be interpreted, our minds even

impose limits to our experience: if we have a small vessel, we can't get much water. The mind will take just a little bit of understanding and narrow down the experience by its understanding. The purpose of meditation is to overcome the limitation of the mind so that we can extend our realization and encompass wider fields of reality.

There are basic techniques for working with consciousness. Consciousness is like eyesight: if you are reading a book, your field of vision is extremely narrow, but if you are contemplating a horizon, you are encompassing a wide field. In exactly the same way, consciousness can be pinpointed on the details of things, or it can be extended to encompass a wide field of reality.

If you walk in the streets of a city, you can't have a very clear idea of the lie of the land, but if you could fly over it in a helicopter you would have a beautiful panoramic view and see how everything is related to everything else. Generally in life, we get ourselves caught up in a certain narrow vision of things. We get stuck in a little groove, and we fail to see the forest for the trees: we are caught in the perspectives of things as they appear to us. Our understanding is limited by the perspective of our consciousness, and in most cases our consciousness is lenslike. It distorts reality by narrowing down the picture of reality into a center, so that what we experience is not reality but the way reality looks from the point of view of that lens. But we also have a holistic or holographic way of looking at things that is latent within our understanding. Just as we can see three dimensions when we use both eyes together, somehow behind our idea of the appearance of objects there is a feeling of the interrelationship in a whole pattern. We continually shuttle between these two perspectives, but the main perspective is looking at things as though they were the way they seem.

Those moments when our consciousness extends into the

panoramic dimension and we begin to see the whole are the great moments, when all of a sudden everything enters into perspective, because we see the relationship between what we were experiencing before and the totality. At those moments, there is also a change in our notion of ourself and our notion of identity. We lose our sense of being a person different from other people, and our notion of ourselves merges with others. We experience ourselves as part of one being. This is, of course, the experience of the Sufis—experiencing the One Being of which one is a part instead of thinking of oneself as a definite, separate individual. Sufis call this *fana*. The frontier between oneself and the environment seems to fade out, and there is a feeling of belonging to the totality. There is no way of saying it; it is just a sense of reality beyond the way things appear, and it is the only thing that saves us from the despair and loneliness of the self. There is a kind of tyranny of the ego: we suffer by our own sense of ourselves. We may not realize it, but we are stifled by our own sense of individuality, and it is wonderful to be able to be free even for just one moment from that terrible tyranny and to have a wonderful sense of the reality behind all that.

We can actually work with consciousness and extend consciousness in the vastness on purpose. Just as people living in cities are used to very narrow perspectives, Tibetans, for example, who sit on the tops of mountains, are used to looking at enormous, widespread panoramic scenes. Our whole way of thinking can become very sclerosed by the pressure of society and of civilization; we can become little persons using only middle-range thinking. In fact, scientifically we know that our ordinary way of thinking is within the middle ranges of understanding. As soon as we reach the wide ranges of understanding, things appear very different.

There is also a way of working with consciousness by extending it inside instead of outside. For example, you could experience what it is like to be a tree instead of looking at a tree from your own perspective. If you simply look at a tree, all you are seeing is the bark of the tree from a certain angle—you are not really seeing the tree. In fact, you will never really know the tree; it is like ships passing in the night. The only way you could know the tree would be to enter into its consciousness and experience what it is like to be a tree. The same thing is also true of a dog. How well do we know our dog? Do we know what we look like to him? We are used to thinking of him as just a dog—and maybe his greatest problem is just being a dog. Perhaps he would like us to be able to understand how he thinks. In fact, we *can* understand how he thinks, but it takes a certain effort on our part. This consists of being able to transpose our consciousness from its normal vantage point and place it in what we call the "object."

In reality, there is no such thing as "subject" and "object." This is just our way of thinking, because we think in terms of being centered in our particular selves and assume that consciousness functions from the vantage point of the body. In fact, consciousness can very well be transferred from the body. At those moments when we feel a part of nature, our consciousnes is not limited in the body; we are really merging into the landscape. In the same way, it is possible for consciousness to enter the consciousness of various beings and experience what it is like to be them. This is a very common practice among the Sufis, and I think it is probably what Martin Buber meant by the "I-Thou" relationship as opposed to the "I-It" relationship. Normally we are so enclosed in our personal perspective that we don't even know we are not experiencing things the way they are. When we suddenly realize that there is another way of looking at things, a whole new horizon opens up.

Perhaps one of the most helpful things is to get into the

consciousness of a master—a realized being—because to become what we are we have to see ourselves in another "ourself." What we think we are, which is what we assume is our personality, is only a very small fraction of what we are. Behind that is a whole field of qualities and defects— potentialities that are present but have not yet come into the world of actuality.

One of the best examples of this can be found in the realm of biology. A biologist named W.H. Thorpe has asked how it is that every cell of the body has exactly the same DNA structure. The nucleus of the cell, which is a macromolecule, has exactly the same structure as every other cell, so how is it that one cell becomes hair and another becomes blood and another becomes gray matter? They all have the same structure in their nuclei, basically; the coding is the same. The model Thorpe used was the keyboard of a piano. Each cell is like the keyboard of a piano that has millions of keys, but most of the keys are Scotch-taped so that you can only play a certain melody within certain limits. That is the programming behind it all: that the cell is only allowed to function in a certain way and so produce hair or whatever it is.

The same thing is true of ourselves. We have absolutely everything in us, but we are only using some of the potentialities within our being. How these have all been programmed is very complex and depends upon the environment in which we were brought up, our inheritance, and many other factors. The important thing is that these potentialities can be released into actuality at any moment. They are not Scotch-taped forever. You just have to pull off the Scotch tape. It is simply a matter of realization: when you realize your inheritance, you become it. This is the whole secret of Christianity. When Christ said, "Be ye perfect as your Father in heaven is perfect," that was what he meant—that all you have to do is become conscious of your inheritance, which is perfect.

In both Judaism and Islam, the question of Christ being the Son of God is very touchy. How could he make that claim? In what way was he different from any other human being? This is a major theological issue. Nowadays, many people realize that these theological problems don't really make sense, because they are just in the mind. Our minds can't grasp these things, and, therefore, we might as well give up the controversy at the mind level. What Hazrat Inayat Khan said, which is very illuminating on this point, is that Christ was able to claim to be the Son of God because he was aware of his inheritance. If you are aware of your divine inheritance, you can claim it. If you think that you are the son of your father, you can only claim to be the son of your father. But there are many different inheritances that come into the formation of your being, and if you are conscious of your divine inheritance, you can manifest it. This is a great secret.

As we said before, in order to be able to discover yourself you have to be able to see yourself in another yourself. We might say that that which takes away the Scotch tape on the keyboards is the ability to recognize the quality you have when you see it in another person. It is easier to see it in another person than to see it in yourself. Occasionally—more typically in the East, and not so much nowadays as before—you come across a being who is just like a king. Not a political king, but a real king—a being who has great sovereignty and great inner power, realization and wisdom, light and magnetism. In India when I was younger, I came across some incredible beings. Our civilization somehow makes it difficult for people to reach the degree of perfection that is to be found among people living in caves—which is a terrible reflection on our civilization. One could even say that the dervish is the product of a way of thinking and of living that is almost extinct nowadays. But if you do see a being like that, you discover yourself in that being.

I was quite young when I had my first encounter with a great rishi sitting in a cave. I had come a long way. I had walked three days and three nights in the snow, and I had caught pneumonia. I was also rather scared, because there were tracks in the snow that I thought might be the tracks of a bear, and bears are quite dangerous in the Himalayas. I followed the tracks anyway, in the hope that they were the footsteps of a human being, and they turned out to be the tracks of a rishi. The first thing he said to me was, "Why have you come so far to see what you should be?" I was still rather inexperienced, so I just said, "It is wonderful to see this." Today, I suppose I would have said, "To become what I should be I have to see myself in you."

When you watch a sunrise, the light—the colors of the light and the glory and majesty of the sun that come through the spectrum of colors—can have a traumatic action upon you, leading to the sudden realization that it is what you are yourself. That is why you like it: because you *are* it. You recognize yourself in that glorious sunshine, and at that moment you become luminous. This is an encounter with a reality that is already present in yourself. But imagine getting into the consciousness of the sun instead of just watching the sun from your vantage point! In the same way, if you are sitting in the presence of a rishi, you can experience what it is like to *be* a rishi instead of experiencing just sitting there in front of him. This is a totally different experience—and the most wonderful experience you could have. When you come out of that state—that experience—you are totally transformed. You are the rishi. You can walk in the street and see everyone caught up in their personal consciousness, and you know they are just caught in a certain perspective, and that you have been freed from that perspective by your encounter with the rishi or the dervish. That's the meaning of spiritual life.

It is also the reason for what has become perhaps too much of a custom in the East: losing oneself in a teacher. This is fine if the teacher is really a totally realized being, but if he is not, then it is very dangerous. In fact, according to Islam, it is only God to whom one should ultimately submit, and not to any human being. We know from the experience in Guyana a few years ago what danger there is in just following a person blindly because he tells you what to do. The thing to do is to become able to see the being of God in a person—or the sunrise, or even a dog. That is the real meaning of the *dhikr*, the mantram "La illaha illa 'llah hu" ("Nothing exists save God"), which is the affirmation of the unity of God in all things; and this is, of course, the point of view of the Sufis. If you adopt their point of view, you can no longer look at a rishi as if you were you and he were himself. You have to enter into his being. If all is one Being, there is only one consciousness, and entering into the consciousness of the rishi or the dervish is just the first step leading to a further step, which is entering into the divine consciousness. That is the ultimate of Sufism: continually being conscious of the divine consciousness.

Two stages in the Sufi path are *fana-fi-shaikh* and *fana-fi-Allah*. In the first, you are able to enter into the consciousness of a wonderful being, the shaikh or spiritual leader. But this being is in fact only the exemplification of the totality—the One Being, Allah, who is coming through in a particular way that is appealing to you.

David Bohm, a professor of physics in London, has made experiments with ink drops placed in glycerine. When they are rolled between two cylinders, they disappear; you can't see them anymore. Bohm calls this the implicate state. If you roll them back again, all of a sudden they reappear in the opposite order in which they were placed in the glycerine. This is the explicate state. Bohm says that all physical reality is like this. What we experience is that aspect or condition of reality that has transpired, or emerged as the droplets—the explicate state—but there is a whole realm of reality that we don't normally experience, which is in the implicate state and thus beyond the grasp of our senses. The lenslike nature of our senses can apprehend only a certain fraction or perspective of reality.

The same thing is true of our thinking. Our minds have a tendency to turn in circles when considering a problem. You may say, "Okay, it's all right, I am going to do this." And then all of a sudden you think it over and say, "No, I can't do that." Then you may decide to go back to your first decision, and then change your mind again. The reason for this is that the mind is unable to grasp the whole problem, so when you are considering a problem it will bring out certain aspects which then become clear to you. They come into focus, like a slide projected on a screen. You can bring a slide into focus and then think you can see the object. In fact, what is present on the screen when it is out of focus is much richer than when it is in focus. It is limited by being in focus, but you can grasp it because it corresponds to the scope of your consciousness. When we bring a problem into focus, we see a certain aspect of the problem clearly, but there are others that are out of focus. When we bring another aspect into focus, the first one is out of focus. It takes training of the consciousness to be able to incorporate all the aspects of the problem into one big holistic view.

Our consciousness has a certain amount of scope, and it can be focused in this or that direction. We can increase the scope so that it can be both implicate and explicate at the same time. There is always some implicit thinking in our explicit thinking—thoughts that are in the background and are not very clear while we are thinking. When you think of a person, your thought about that person includes a lot of things, like your memory of having met him or her, a conversation you may have had, or even the clothes he or she wore. There are a lot of things to think of, and most of them are not very clear. You can try to remember: "Did he have a long nose or a short nose?" Or, "What was the color of her eyes?" You can bring certain aspects into focus—but then the other aspects are out of focus. Or you can try to encompass the whole general feeling of the person, but at the moment you do that you can't be very clear about certain explicit parts of the person. In the same way, you can consider a whole problem, but then you don't see any part of it clearly; you see only the interrelationships between the problems. So the important thing is to be able to see the interrelationships *and also* the details. And that requires, of course, an increase in the scope of consciousness.

So one could say that in meditation we are working with consciousness to increase its scope, and that this is something that is in some ways related to our sense of ourselves. If you think of yourself as being your personality, you are identifying yourself with the explicate aspect of your being and refusing to see the whole enormous field of reality that you are. The consequence of this is that your consciousness will be limited. As soon as you begin to recognize your divine inheritance—in other words, to identify yourself with all the potentialities in your being—then your consciousness increases its scope, and you will be looking at problems from a totally different angle. The essence of Buddhism is to be found in these words of Buddha himself: "Consciousness has been carried beyond a point where it is an individual consciousness." In fact, the reason we use the word *Tathagata* when speaking about Buddha is because *tat* means "that" or "thus"; *Tathagata* means "He has become Thus"—i.e., impersonal and not limited by the limitations of individuality.

The extension of consciousness I have been describing so far is in what I call the cosmic dimension. It is this that gives you a sense of vastness. When you come into contact with a great being, you have a feeling of vastness; a great being becomes more cosmic the less individual he becomes. Many of us are suffering from our sense of narrowness and have to gain this sense of vastness. What maintains us in our narrowness is the assumption that we are a fraction of the totality. It is very difficult for our logical mind to accept that we are *both* a fraction of the totality *and also* the totality.

When we make a retreat, we do the Sufi practice of *dhikr*, repeating "La illaha illa 'llah hu." If you did a classical Sufi retreat, it could be forty days of fasting and repeating this mantram from morning until night; and I can assure you that if you do this, something happens to you. You lose your sense of identity; your consciousness is totally transformed in what I call the transcendental dimension. So far as I can see, I can distinguish clearly two dimensions in our experience: the cosmic dimension and the transcendental dimension.

When you experience yourself as being the totality, that is the very limit of the cosmic dimension. We have that experience in a very elementary way when we are young and we lie down on the grass on our backs and look into the sky, and our bodies merge with nature and we just feel like part of it all. We lose our sense of identity and enter into the consciousness of the totality.

The other dimension—the transcendental dimension—is very different. In it, you suddenly realize that you are not your body, not your personality, not your mind, and so on. It is a totally different way of looking at things, and yet both of these experiences are valid. From my personal experience, I know that if you are repeating the *dhikr*, a mantram that says, in essence, "This is not me, there is only one being and that Being is God," and if you don't lose yourself in the words but instead get deeper and deeper into the meaning of the words, you can find yourself looking at your body and thinking, "Isn't that extraordinary. It's just the fabric of the planet; it is the same as the earth and the water, the same as the fabric of the stars. In fact, the earth has detached itself from the sun, so it is the material of the sun. And I think this is me; but how could it be me? It is the substance of the planet." And you can just imagine what has gone into the programming of the universe to have made such a fantastic body.

When you see that your body has emerged out of the substance of the planet, you think, "Now I see myself as a wave that has emerged out of the ocean." But there is a second point of realization when you see that it isn't true to say that your body has emerged from the ocean: it is the ocean that has heaved up into this body. As a matter of fact, the study of physics teaches us that when a wave emerges from the sea, the whole rest of the sea has to adjust itself to it. So you could say that the whole physical universe is involved in the formation of this body. That is the point Teilhard de Chardin made very clearly when he said that we are the convergence of the universe—it has taken the whole universe to make this body. The whole universe is involved, so you can't think that your body is just a fragment of the universe. You have to overcome the idea of yourself as being an entity in itself. The extraordinary thing is that we are able to participate in the universe *that we are ourselves.*

You can experience the same phenomenon at the mind level when you realize that your thinking—or what you thought was your thinking—is in fact the thinking of the universe, which works in a certain way. There is no such thing as personal thinking. It is the universe that is thinking. You can get to a point when you enter into the thinking of the trees, but there is a further stage, and at that stage you look into the thinking that became the tree—the thinking of the universe that manifested itself as a tree.

This is what is meant by entering into the mind of God. It is an extraordinary moment in meditation when all of a sudden you realize that you have access to the thinking of God, of which this physical universe is a kind of projection that is experienced through the senses.

The same thing applies at another level: the level of the personality. This happens when you realize that what you thought was your personality is really an inheritance from an untold number of beings, and that nature has proceeded in this way to form this personality. How can you say it is you? You may say, "Yes, but surely I must have some influence upon it." Indeed you do, in the same way that you have an influence upon your body. Your body may be the product of the forces of nature, but isn't it extraordinary that you are able to make this lump of flesh move? You can't make a tree move. You have a relationship with this particular lump of flesh that you don't have with other parts of the physical universe—although the mere fact that you can make your body move does not prove that you *are* your body.

In both the Hindu and the Buddhist traditions— particularly in the Hindu tradition, which is where it originated—there is an idea of a dichotomy between *prakriti* and *purusha*—between that which is transient and that which is eternal. When you get into the transcendental dimension of meditation, you have the paradoxical thought that you are not your body, not your mind, not your personality, and so on, and you come to the realization that what you are in reality is a visitor from outer space who is visiting the planet for a short time and who has borrowed a body out of the substance of the planet, and even borrowed a personality. You are not this personality at all; just like the body, it is a vehicle that you can use to experience conditions on the planet—and perhaps even to do something about situations on the planet—but even your personality is a formation, and therefore, you are not it. You identify yourself with *purusha*—that which is eternal, or spirit.

However, although we may be able to accept that the body

has been borrowed from the substance of the planet, that the mind has been borrowed from the thinking of the planet, and even that the personality has been inherited and is a formation, we might still like to believe that we are a consciousness. It took the activity of Buddha to realize that even consciousness is not eternal—that even consciousness is subject to change. In fact, consciousness is subject to its object: it depends upon its object.

Imagine a person sitting in the darkness in a sensory-deprivation tank, who can't hear anything and doesn't have any input from the senses, and who is practicing samadhi, so that he is not thinking of any particular subject. Would he still be conscious? Consciousness needs an object to be conscious of. What was consciousness would aver itself to be intelligence. Hazrat Inayat Khan says that intelligence becomes consciousness when it is dealing with an object. If there is an object, there is a dichotomy between consciousness and object, but when there is no object, consciousness returns to its source, which is intelligence. That is a further stage in the experience one has in meditation: you realize that you are pure intelligence—not consciousness, but intelligence. That is the experience of samadhi, which the Sufis call 'al 'ama. In English, one might call it the state of unknowing, or the cloud of unknowing; as Saint John of the Cross said, the light becomes so intense it appears as darkness. I prefer the word "obscurity," because "darkness" tends to give a depressive feeling, whereas what we are describing is just unknowing.

The Hindus make a very beautiful comparison between meditation and sleep. There are several states of sleep, among them what scientists call paradoxical sleep and orthodox sleep. In paradoxical sleep, there are images and dreams, but when you get to a deeper stage in sleep, there are no more images and no more rapid eye movement, which is associated with the dream stage. At this deeper stage, orthodox sleep, there is an awareness without an object. This is the kind of experience we all have in deep sleep—although perhaps we shouldn't use the word "experience," because even that assumes a subject and an object. We might say that we live it in deep sleep, although most of us do not remember it.

There is a technique used in India, called *nidra yoga*, which consists of actually maintaining the continuity of memory in sleep. Imagine that you are on the threshold of dreaming, or paradoxical, sleep. You may remember and even be conscious of the room and the sound of the cars in the street, but even if you are not conscious of these things, you do at least remember the scene of the physical world, your situation in life and so on; these are very clear to you, but at the same time they are shifting images in a state of reverie. There is a kind of overlapping of consciousness at most levels, so you can't influence the images very well, at least not by your personal will, because in order to be able to reach beyond the threshold of ordinary consciousness you have to abandon your sense of your individuality. When you do, you have no individual will and no individual consciousness, and that is why you cannot change your dreams. You may be conscious of the physical world and the images emerging on the screen of your mind, but there is nothing much you can do about it. Nevertheless, the fact that you are able to see them clearly imposes a kind of order on them, which is an amazing thing. And being able to clarify your mind is, exactly, meditation. This is why the Hindus draw a parallel between the experience in sleep and in meditation.

You can even suggest dreams to yourself, and in some way the unconscious mind will take over the suggestion of the conscious mind so that you create dreams: clarity of consciousness will order dreams that would otherwise be chaotic. People who are confused seem to need a lot of dreams, or paradoxical sleep, to sort out their confused energies, whereas people who are clearer in their minds don't need so much paradoxical sleep—they don't need to dream as much. The rishis who practice *nidra yoga* don't sleep at all in the sense of going into a state of total somnolence where one isn't conscious of anything at all and there are just images. They always have a very perfect consciousness of their memory of conditions on the physical plane.

The key to this clarity is to accept that you are not what you thought you were. In a dream, you seem to be a totally different personality than in your everyday consciousness. If you have already overcome your sense of identity, you can accept the dream world, but if you refuse the dream world, your continuity of consciousness is broken when you get into that realm. This is why we don't remember very much of our dreams. If you are able to accept that you are not what you thought you were in your diurnal consciousness, then you can enter into the dream world and discover the thoughts of all creativity.

Most of our thinking is a reaction instead of an action: we are continually dealing with the input from outside. There are very few thoughts that are totally creative. One could say that the creative thoughts are thoughts that descend upon us from what Hazrat Inayat Khan calls the "storehouse of all knowledge," which can come through in dreams. Artists and musicians are in communication with this inspiration that has arrived from a kind of dream world. So access to the dream world is very important.

The next stage is reaching into orthodox sleep, where there are no images anymore. Imagine that you have arrived at a very high degree of understanding of meaningfulness, but there is nothing to describe—it is like the meaningfulness behind the meaningfulness of the meaningfulness. This is a kind of reflective understanding. Teilhard de Chardin said that animals think, but the human being knows that he thinks

—which is a further degree of understanding. In the same way, samadhi is not thinking, but a further degree of realization: realizing that one realizes.

This is the realm of transcendence. When you have crossed the threshold of the realm of transcendence, you can see very clearly that you had let yourself be caught in the perspective of your individuality, and that it is in fact only a perspective. It is very clear that while everything seems to be happening in time and space, it is really only a projection: reality is beyond whatever is happening in the realm of existence. What you are experiencing is, as Buddha says, beyond existence. Once you have experienced this, you can never be the same. You have seen behind the curtain. This is what the Sufis call awakening.

Why is it that you are changed? Because from that time on you cannot be fooled anymore. For example, in your relationships with people you see very clearly how you let yourself be caught up in their trips and so lose your freedom—not only your freedom of action, but your freedom of thinking and even your freedom of realization. Most of us are what are called householders in the East, rather than sannyasins, or renunciates. We have responsibilities—our families, our jobs, and so on. We can't afford just to live in meditation all the time. We are involved, which means we have to abandon our freedom—to give of our freedom graciously in order to free people by binding ourselves to them. This is very challenging: do you dare free people by abandoning your freedom and at the same time maintain a kind of inner freedom?

Despite the fact that most of us are involved in life, there is something of the ascetic in each of us: we are both the hermit and the knight. Even people who entertain a very high spiritual ideal must be both. You are a hermit in the sense that although you are in the world, you are not of it, as Christ said; and you are a knight in the sense that you are acting in the world in order to bring about some change. In fact, the whole point of action is to bring about change, even if only in a very material way, such as building a house. Most action, however, is not so much with matter as with people. The important questions are, "What do I do to people, and what do they do to me? What do I mean to people? What do they mean to me? Am I binding them or imposing my wishes upon them? Or am I giving up my spirituality to them? Am I able to uphold my ideal, or am I compromising my ideals?"

From the moment you can extend your consciousness into the consciousness of all beings, you are able to understand them in a way you could never understand them before. For example, when I look into the hearts of people, I see so much suffering there. People feel they have been badly dealt with by other people, if not by destiny—which is a polite way of saying "God," but people say "destiny" because they don't like to think God did something to them. The feeling of having been dealt with unfairly and the grudge against people build a kind of bitterness, and, of course, judgment. But from the moment you enter into the divine consciousness, you realize that the person who might have ruined your life was just a stick with which God hit you, or nudged you, or brought you out of your complacency. He was only an instrument. So you don't blame the person anymore. The axiom is that you may be judgmental about an action, but never about a person. The important thing is to understand what it is that God is trying to tell you in what the person is doing to you. What is God trying to convey to you? If you just have a grudge against the person, you are not learning anything. Things don't just happen accidentally. Maybe you have to learn how to forgive the person. And maybe if you forgive him, he'll stop bugging you —or maybe he'll continue to bug you. But if you do whatever you have to do, whether it's forgiving the person or becoming more in control of yourself, or whatever it is, the curious thing is that even if the situation doesn't change, it doesn't worry you anymore. The change has taken place in yourself. You realize that the situation had to be there to bring about that change in yourself. This is what the programming is all about: that we should improve.

We want to understand meaningfulness, and it is very clear that in our ordinary setting of consciousness we can't understand it. It is only in that moment when our understanding is carried beyond its limits that we realize what an extraordinary privilege is ours to be able to participate in the whole—not only that our thought is part of the divine thinking, but that in our little field we are able by our action to participate in the evolution of the universe. However narrow our field may be, we are all contributing toward something very important.

We are living in very troubled times. We have sinned against Mother Earth, polluting her, and there are problems for which we don't know the solution—or, if we know the solution, it is difficult to apply it. We are not up to the understanding that is needed to control the situation on the planet. The only way of dealing with this is to raise the consciousness of humankind in our time. There is no other way. Our level of consciousness is not up to the immensity of the problem that we are dealing with at present. We have to find a new way of spirituality that is in keeping with the measure of our times. That is the meaning of the message of Sufism. It is the message for our time.

CHAPTER 2

# The Wine of the Divine Sacrament

There is nothing more soul-killing than to be low-key:
there's a need to be high. The word used by the dervishes is
"intoxicated"; Hazrat Inayat Khan calls it "the wine of the
divine sacrament." This is what ecstasy is: being carried to the
heights by something overwhelming and beyond yourself. It's
the most important thing, the thing that will transform your
life. One can't live on bread alone; one also needs wine. You
can't really achieve anything in cold blood, just as you can't
transform iron unless it's molten. You can't even realize
things in cold blood. It takes emotion to be able to
understand.

So there is a need to dance the cosmic joy of Shiva. Yet we
seem to have cut the possibility of doing it out of our lives and
to have fed ourselves with ersatz pleasures. We sacrifice joy for
pleasure, and try to entertain ourselves with very puny things
indeed—things that are really very soul-killing. The real

breakthrough of joy only happens when we are moved to the core of our being—when we are shattered by our encounter with meaningfulness.

Joy is the breakthrough of freedom: it's when you are free from your ego consciousness that you are really happy. Being free, of course, does not necessarily mean not being bound by a job or family or social conventions. The real freedom is freedom from the conditioning of the lower self. We all have a real longing for real freedom, which is the moment in which consciousness becomes all-encompassing and we feel part of the universe. We also long for that other experience of having gone beyond manifestation into *parat param*—"beyond the beyond"—which is the highest form of meditation.

Yet we mustn't think that this is the objective. It's wonderful to reach that pinnacle, but the trend of our time is to bring meditation to bear on the reality of everyday living. Imagine that you were in a state of awakening and realization and illumination and joy in the middle of doing the most ordinary things! The word "awakening" is very important, because one only knows what awakening is when one awakens, of course; one doesn't realize that one is sleeping. Most people do not remember the awareness they had when they were dreaming, but if you could remember when you got back into ordinary consciousness the awareness you had when you were dreaming, you would realize that when you were dreaming, the physical world seemed like a dream, and that in fact you had a feeling of awakening from a dream.

Now, that is exactly the spiritual objective: awakening. Imagine that you are completely awake among people who are sleeping. You think to yourself, "Isn't it extraordinary that I should have been asleep. I thought things were the way they seemed to me, and now I see that they are not the way they seem to be. And people are still in the place where I was—they still look at things from the point of view of one who is asleep.

And now that I am awake, I can see that most people are asleep around me." It sounds very bumptious to say a thing like that, and one probably shouldn't say it; but if you are awake, you can't help realizing that something has really happened to you.

There are, of course, many dimensions to awakening. For example, you see why things happen the way they do, and you can imagine how one might be continually struggling with the mind to try to understand things—and this is why, in the New Age, people are fed up with the reasoning of philosophers. That's why the greatest advice ever given me was from a dervish who said, "Only speak when you realize that you can't say what you want to say. If you think you can say it, then don't say it." Language is very imperfect. For example, many people say "Him" when speaking of God. In our language, "Him" means someone other than ourselves. That's the reason why people are so antagonistic about religious formulations—because they go counter to their own deep intuitive sense and bring people instead into a whole construction of mental concepts.

So we live in a world of concepts, but in order to be able to awaken you have to overcome the concepts. You have to shatter all that you ever thought and find yourself in direct contact with reality. Then you have to build a new kind of pigeonhole system in order to account for what you have experienced—the old system just won't do anymore. That's what I mean by blowing your mind. You don't have room in your mind to absorb reality, because it is presented with such strength that you don't have the capacity for it.

This is, of course, the point the Sufis are making when they say that if you could ever look into the sun, your eyes would be burned, and if you could ever understand the reality of things, your understanding would be completely shattered. This is what happened to Saint John of the Cross when he went through the dark night of the soul. First he had to go through the dark night of the understanding: all the things he had believed in had been based on thoughts, and all those thoughts were being shattered. And there he was without any support at all for his thinking.

Imagine that you can't use your mind anymore to think, because it's too imperfect a computer to be able to serve your purpose. This is what happens, and it's the only thing that can really help us to get away from all those things that are holding us in subjection by their power. We're not only conditioned, but really bullied by the mental stuff that we've received in the course of years and that we take for granted— and are rebelling against.

Somehow, then, there is that moment of life when there is communication of life with life instead of with words or concepts. Life always triggers off life wherever it goes, love triggers off love, and joy triggers off joy. These are very real things: that moment when time stands still and you feel you are talking to a person beyond time and space. All of a sudden you see into the soul of the person, and it is as if a veil were lifted and you're really high at that moment: you get into a real, deep communion with that person and you realize yourselves as a part of a greater Person. Then that greater Person becomes a real awareness instead of just a concept of God.

It's easy to understand why people rebel against a concept of God, because it's very chilling. In fact, Hazrat Inayat Khan said that it is the concept men have made of God that has stood in the way of the faith of many people, because people build a kind of barrier between humanity and God, thinking of God as other and as Him. So we have to think very differently, and perhaps we must use the word "Us" when we think of God, instead of "Him." And by "Us," we must mean not just humans, but all the animals and the angels and the pixies and the archangels, the atoms and the planets, and so on. The living experience, of course, affects all one's thinking. In science, whenever a scientist comes across a new phenomenon that doesn't fit into the theories that have been elaborated so far, he or she has to formulate a newer theory. This is what happened to Einstein, and is, in fact, the reason for the tremendous breakthrough of modern science. Einstein just refused to take things that were told him for granted, and so freed himself to look at things from another angle.

In the same way, there is a need to approach spiritual problems from a new angle. The classical way of liberation is to liberate yourself from your point of view and from the circumstances of life that bind you and therefore confine you. This is the way of the sannyasin or the rishi. But then you might think, "Isn't it the height of selfishness to want to be free when everybody else is involved in all kinds of situations? Is that the purpose of life? Isn't it to live life deeply and fully that we came on earth?" Then you understand that saying of the Sufi poet Attar, who said, "Renounce the good of the world, renounce your highest ideal, and then renounce renunciation."

These are real paradoxical challenges, and we are meeting them all along the path: there is a new vision of spirituality. We knock at the doors of the rishis and the dervishes and ask them for a solution to our problems in life, and at first they say, "Leave everything and become a sannyasin and you'll see." But now the dervish leaves his cave or his little hole in the wall and comes to New York.

In order to progress, you have to renounce what you valued before; otherwise you stay where you were. This is the secret of developing power that is used by the rishis. For example, if you're hungry, you don't eat; if you're sleepy, you don't sleep; and if you're cold, you simply keep on sitting there in the snow meditating, as I've seen some of them do. You become really very strong: if a person spits in your face, you kiss his feet.

And if everything breaks down around you, you dance for joy.

This is the most powerful thing that can happen to you: to arrive at a point where nothing can affect you because you are free. And you don't have to go into a cave to come to that point. On the contrary, it is much more challenging to do it in everyday life. For instance, renunciation doesn't mean not to love; it means to love without expecting to be loved in return.

Of course, most people feel dissatisfied with modern living. They feel they've been caught up in a system that has tricked them. For instance, the people in the typing pool may realize that it's because of their labor that the boss can have his house in Miami. And there's a point where people realize that the competition of pushing each other aside to get into each other's places is soul-killing, and most of us can't cope with it anymore because we realize that this is not what we're looking for. And we may also realize that we're subject to tremendous exploitation by big firms like those involved in food processing, which have caused us to go so far from the real things that an organic potato is one of the most expensive things you can buy.

**Spirituality, for our purposes, is not just a matter of applying the principles of spirituality to everyday life, but** really transforming life by the realization that we attain by reaching spiritual realization. We're beginning to intuit a guidance behind what we do. And then, finally, we discover that there is nothing in life that isn't programmed—and, what is more, the programming is not the effect of the past. It is continually spontaneous. What we think are the laws are simply the fossilization of divine freedom. The law is the past, but the effect of the future is free. Freedom is just a matter of realizing that you are free. All the time that you thought you were not free, you were in fact free—you just didn't know it. And because you didn't know it, you weren't. It's simply a matter of realization. We could build a wonderful world and we could all become wonderful people—and what is more, we should. And we will.

CHAPTER 3

# The Call of the Dervish

Let's say you have a chat with some friends, and they tell you something about the Sufis. You think to yourself, "It sounds far out; I'd like to know more about the Sufis." They say, "The typical Sufi is the dervish, someone who really acts very strongly on your being and tries to awaken you." "What does that mean, to awaken?" "Well, if you'd like to be awakened, try to go and see a dervish."

"But how do I see a dervish?" "Why don't you go to India, to Ajmer—the center of Mu'in ad-din Chishti?" So you look at the map, and you look at your bank account; you have a few days' holiday coming up, so you book a flight for Delhi. You have a traumatic shock, of course—let's say a cultural shock—even apart from the speed of the taxi driving and things like that. You think, "Let's get to Ajmer as quickly as possible." You take the overnight train, and in the morning you encounter all the *khadims*—the guardians of the tomb of Mu'in ad-din Chishti—who come and say, "Are you looking for the *dargah* of Khawaja Mu'in ad-din Chishti?" "Yes, yes." "Well, come with me." And another one says, "No, no, no, don't go with him, come with me." One is pulling you one way and the other has your luggage, and then there's a cabman approaching with his horse and cart and saying, "No, take a taxi." You think, "Oh, no, what have I come to?" So you choose one of the *khadims,* generally the one who's the most pushy.

You land in what may once have been a minor castle but is now a real backwater slum, and you think, "Well, I suppose this is the only place I can stay." Anyway, you say, "Can you take me to the *dargah*?" "Yes, yes, we could go tomorrow." You have the whole day in front of you. You say, "Can't we go now?" "You rest, just rest. I'll bring you a cup of tea." So you just sit there. Then you think, "I'll get my sleeping bag ready," and you try to brush a bit of space clear, amidst the dust and cockroaches and the other beasties, and you finally lie down to sleep.

In the middle of the night there's a knock at the door. You hear a very mysterious kind of voice. You're terrified and you pull the covers over the top of your head. Then the whole door begins to shake, and you get a cold chill in your back. Then you hear the voice going farther away, so you feel a bit relieved. But then all of a sudden it occurs to you that that might have been the very dervish you're looking for. "Too late. I came all this way and missed it. But then maybe it wasn't a dervish—how do I know?"

In the morning, the *khadim* comes with a cup of tea. You tell him your story, and he says, "Oh, yes, that's the dervish. He comes to wake people up at three in the morning." "Oh, I missed him. So, can I go to the *dargah* today?" "Yes, yes, I'll take you." By eleven o'clock you're at the *dargah*—and there isn't a dervish in sight. You think, "What a pity I missed that opportunity."

That night you go to sleep again, and at three o'clock there's the inevitable shaking of the door. You think, "This time I'm really going to get up." By the time you're dressed, he's already gone. So you follow in the dark streets, trying to remember the way to the *dargah* and to avoid the dogs barking at you and keep them from getting close enough to bite. Finally you reach the *dargah* and sit there in a kind of enchantment. It's incredible. A few bodies turn in their sleep, someone is saying prayers in the mosque, someone else is singing. It's incredible, and you just sit there and feel very happy.

You feel a presence behind you, and you hear the same voice that you heard through the door. You dare not turn around, because it really gets very strong. But all of a sudden that being is in front of you, and you just don't believe it. He's dressed in an old mattress. He's got about ten rings on each hand. He looks more far-out than you could possibly imagine. He's got eyes of fire, and he looks at you and says, "*You there.*" You're completely nonplussed—you can't think what to say. Before you know what's happened, he goes somewhere else. You try to recover from the shock and follow him, but by that time he's lost in a crowd. Then you realize that you came to India just for that moment when he said, "*You there.*" What did he do at that moment? Somehow he awakened you, and you'll never be the same afterwards. That's the way of the dervish: he awakens you.

It's all part of the encounter with something that is so strong that it transforms you, shatters you in your sense of yourself, perplexes you. "Perplexity" is a key word: it's something that you can't fathom—you can't work it out. It's so challenging to your way of thinking that it leaves a mark on you and you can never be the same. You feel that you have awakened, and you think, "How is it possible that I should have let myself be caught up in all those trips?" It's an awakening from the state of consciousness in which you were.

And what is the power of the dervish? What is really the

essential power of Sufism? It's the power of ecstasy. The reason the dervish has such a strong action on you is that he is in a state of intoxication beyond what you could ever imagine. Everyone is in some kind of state of intoxication, but there are different kinds of wine. Some people like *vin ordinaire*, some like Chateauneuf du Pape, and some prefer champagne. When you were a child, you were intoxicated by your toys. You couldn't sleep if you didn't have your doll or your teddy bear. Then, when you grew up, you gave up that kind of intoxication and sought other forms of intoxication, like being in love, or studying music, or wanting to learn something about whatever interested you. There are lots of intoxications people can be subject to: football, stamp collecting, skiing, hang gliding—in fact, the whole of life is intoxicating. We can't live on bread alone, we need wine—something that is really meaningful to us, that will really turn us on, that will give us zest to galvanize all our energy. The worst thing that could happen to you is to be low-key—when there's nothing that turns you on. Ecstasy is always experienced in being carried beyond yourself, whether it's football, rock-and-roll, parachuting, mountain climbing, or whatever—it's something that carries you beyond yourself, an experience that is shattering to your notion of yourself. It might be challenging to your courage; it might be feeling a part of the whole of nature. Anything that makes you lose your confinement in your ego-consciousness and makes you feel part of something greater than yourself—that's what ecstasy is.

There are different situations that can bring you to it. For example, looking at the sunrise in the mountains, or the smile of a child, or the experience of someone asking forgiveness of you or of you asking forgiveness of someone else: these are all things that will give you ecstasy. You are moved in the depths of your being; you are transformed by that experience. It may occur in an encounter with a wonderful being or the discovery of yourself in another being or the discovery of the presence of God. It's seeing meaningfulness where you didn't see it before, like a child looking at a puzzle. "Can you see that little pixie in the tree?" "No, daddy, I can't see it." "Look again." "Yes—I can see it!" Eureka! That's the moment of ecstasy: when you see something you couldn't see before.

There are other forms of ecstasy, which Hazrat Inayat Khan describes. For example, seeing the cause behind a situation; or realizing that your mind is the mind of God and that your understanding is something that's happening to the One Being; or discovering in yourself the power that moves the universe. Or, he says, you can "experience the condition of the spheres." What does that mean? It means feeling the power of life on the planet, or even beyond the planet if you're looking at the stars. It's discovering the life behind this whole scene of life, or the thought behind the whole scene, or the emotion behind the whole scene—the divine emotion behind everything that happens in the universe. The greatest ecstasy is discovering the divine emotion. For example, experiencing the emotion of Bach when he wrote his toccatas and fugues. You enjoy listening to the music, but can you imagine what emotion he experienced writing it? That's sharing in divine emotion.

These are things that are so powerful that you can never be the same after you've experienced them. This is the way of the Sufi: the way of ecstasy. It's being carried beyond your emotion into an emotion that is cosmic, a divine emotion. It's exactly the opposite of being low-key. The strongest thing that can ever happen to you is to be infused with the ecstasy of a being. Ecstasy is contagious, and it's the greatest gift there is. What greater gift can you give people than to confer ecstasy upon them? It's like a *hostia*—a divine host that is handed to you. I remember once having heard that the B Minor Mass of

Bach was being played in a church in Paris; as usual, I had a
lecture, but I tried to catch the end of it. I was too late. But it
was unbelievable just to see the people who were leaving and
rushing into the subway: you could see that they were all
caught up in the ecstasy of what they had experienced.

We must not confuse ecstasy with joy, although it sounds
very much like it. It's something else: there's a combination of
joy and pain in it. It's the joy that arises out of a broken heart.
One has to have known suffering to be able to know joy, and
what is more, one must be able to continue to experience
suffering while experiencing joy. Otherwise it's too unreal.
Just enjoying things leaves something out. It's the combination of joy and suffering that makes for ecstasy. That's why
the Sufi uses the words *fana* and *baqa*—annihilation on the
one hand, and on the other re-creation in the divine consciousness. They call it subsistence. It's the story of the priest in the
concentration camp who had been beaten and who
experienced a greater ecstasy than ever before when he
celebrated his mass. It's Jesus among the Romans.

In fact, Hazrat Inayat Khan speaks of ecstasy as
experiencing God's suffering from the limitation in which He
has to function on the earth plane. It's that moment when
you're captured by the limitation of circumstances and it
doesn't take away your sense of the divine perfection. You can
keep your head high when you're being humiliated, for
example: you experience the divine perfection in the middle of
limitation instead of identifying yourself with your personality. It's very strong; in fact, I would say that the only thing
that helps one to stand pain is to experience it as the
crucifixion of God that you are partaking of.

Hazrat Inayat Khan says, "Those who are given liberty by
Him to act freely are nailed on the earth; and those who are
free to act as they choose on the earth will be nailed in the
heavens." It's paradoxical, like his saying that "Divinity is

human perfection and humanity is divine limitation." It's always paradoxical: when you think you understand, you really don't. That's why they say that the Sufi is wrecked in his body, his mind is blown, and his heart is broken—that's why he's so full of joy; and his soul is wrecked, and that's why he's so full of self-confidence; he becomes pure spirit. That's ecstasy. I imagine Christ must have experienced an incredible ecstasy on the cross, as he appears in that statue that shows him dancing on the cross. That really says it: the victory of the human spirit over the tribulations of the human condition gives ecstasy. It's the victory of your soul against the fiasco of circumstances. It's the opposite of having success in circumstances and losing your soul, as Christ said.

If everything goes right, and you're celebrating because you've become the president of your club, or whatever, that's the worst thing that could happen to you, whereas being jubilant when everything breaks down around you is the most wonderful thing that could happen to you. That's the victory in the middle of the fiasco. And that's the condition of the Sufi: he sees everything breaking down and is so jubilant as it breaks down. There was a lady who came to me and said, "Everything in my life has broken down." I was in a flippant mood, and I said to her, "Best thing that could happen to you." She was really insulted. I didn't mean it as an insult; I felt, that's enough to really give you courage in life, I hope. It's what Hazrat Inayat Khan calls the loss that avers itself to be a gain and the gain that avers itself to be a loss.

So the ecstasy of the Sufi—the intoxication of the Sufi— comes from his particular type of wine. The great Sufi poet Hafiz said, "If those pious ones of long robes listen to my song, they will immediately begin to get up and dance . . . . Forgive me, O pious ones, for I am drunk just now!" The dervish says, "If I can't dance, what can I do?" Intoxication is a state in which one participates in the dance of Shiva—and yet the highest intoxication, curiously enough, is sobriety. That's peace instead of joy. Can you imagine what the intoxication of peace is? The state of Buddha, for example: it's the highest emotion. He said that it's like a sword that cuts through the air and is so strong that nothing can touch it. Peace is the strongest thing there is.

That is a state in which one has overcome all things. It's a particular quality of thinking: you realize that everything is just the way it should be. It's strange, because normally you see all the cruelty and the disasters happening, and you can't say that things are the way they should be. It's very strange to have this outlook that you get at a certain level of realization, when you realize that it has to be the way it is. You begin to understand it. That's the reason for the words of both Christ and Buddha at the end of their lives: "It is fulfilled," and "That which had to be done has been done."

This understanding gives you the incentive to go ahead. You feel that there's this to do and that to do, and if you didn't have the incentive you wouldn't do anything. If you have incentive, it's because behind you there is the divine motivation—the sense of fulfillment that is like the horizon beyond your own horizon. One always thinks that the purpose is at the end, like the horizon toward which you are moving. It's very difficult to understand that the purpose is already fulfilled. It's fulfilled beyond time. That's difficult to understand because we think in terms of time, but in fact the fulfillment of the divine plan is already there, but beyond time—in the infinity of time in the future.

That is the point of view that gives you peace. Otherwise, you are motivated by nostalgia—always longing for that which is not. It is difficult to understand that in God there should be the nostalgia, which is the motivation behind everything that is happening in the course of evolution, and at the same time the satisfaction of knowing that it's all right as it is because it's all already fulfilled. It's like thinking of God as being static and dynamic at the same time, and it is hard to understand. But that is the reason why there are moments when you experience an extraordinary intoxication—when you feel free in yourself, when you feel detached. Nothing can touch you, nothing can affect you, you're free from yourself. That's the moment of sobriety: there's no more longing, there's no more nostalgia, there's no more division. That is what is called *moksha*—liberation—and that is the purpose of Buddhism. There are cycles in our lives: there are moments when there's motivation to reach up to a certain point, and there are moments when you reach the *kemal* state, which is the state in which everything is perfect as it is.

Finally, we want to make a distinction between euphoria and ecstasy. This is a distinction many people can't make. Euphoria is a form of excitement that is intoxicating, like going to a football game and getting all excited: that's euphoria, not ecstasy. We might call euphoria the lowest form of ecstasy. The highest ecstasy is the state of sobriety. Between the two there are all kinds of stages; just as each person stands in life in the place corresponding to his degree of realization, each person is in life in accordance with the kind of wine he enjoys, which means the quality of ecstasy that he really seeks. There are some people who seek vulgar ecstasy. Others seek a very refined and sublime form of ecstasy. It's a matter of evolution. You can't change a person; in time, the person will change. People change in their sense of values, and you can see it in their manner, their way of dressing and their way of speaking, their way of moving and sitting, the type of music they like, and the house they like to live in. You can see the way a person is by all these things. There's a time when people like frills and artificial things, and there are times when they can only stand genuine things. There is a time when you need the snow and the ice: you can't even stand lush flowers and fruit, because you must have something very austere. The same is true in music: sometimes you seek music that is really very austere, and sometimes you like opera. It's all a matter of attunement.

## A MEDITATION ON ECSTASY

*Toward the One: make your soul as high as you can reach; extend your consciousness to incorporate and embrace the entire universe. Make your heart like an ocean of love, encompassing all beings by its breadth, its depths, and its all-accommodating compass. Extend the roots of your being right down into the fabric of the universe. Shake away all the trammels that curtail your freedom—freedom of thought, freedom of understanding—so that you may awaken to cosmic consciousness. Let your heart be lifted by your intuition and your divine beauty, which have been buried under the layers of make-believe and illusion in which we have been caught in our everyday picture of the world. Recover the memory of what you have always been since the beginning of time—what you are and always will be beyond time—and watch the forward march of becoming unfolding itself beneath you while you remain suspended, immobile in eternity, in a state of immunity from agitation and emotional turmoil. Take the wings of independence and detachment: on these wings you can take flight. They are the way to freedom. They give access to the planes beyond your normal purview, so that you may leave your body behind to take care of itself. Leave your body consciousness behind; leave your mind behind. Let your consciousness of the mind take care of the mind, of the thoughts, until you are able to see without eyes and hear without ears and walk without feet and understand without the mind—and experience the ecstasy of cosmic beauty in the soul rather than wallow in the emotions of the heart.*

*Let your understanding be annihilated in the mystery of the unknown. Face the reality that cannot be grasped with the mind by letting yourself be shattered; enjoy the shattering of your being in its encounter with a reality so glorious, so all-encompassing, that we have no measure with which to account for it. We have no means of grasping it except by allowing ourselves to be totally annihilated by it, thereby being resurrected with a power we never knew: the power that runs the universe, the power behind the giddy rotations of the planets and the galaxies and the great spirals of stardust in the heavens; the force within the atom and the force within the sap of the plant; the force that is carrying you forward towards unknown horizons. Be part of it all so that the power of God inhabits you, transforming and strengthening you beyond any conception—and then rise to an ever-wider consciousness so that when you look back upon your life, your little problems and your little concepts, you realize how you've been caught up in the whirlwind of an illusion. How is it possible that you can let yourself be browbeaten into accepting the evidence of the immediate environment when the universe is speaking from its far corners, telling you that what you think you are is simply the crossroads where every atom of the universe meets every other—a juncture, a knot in a network whose end cannot be found?*

*The secret of increasing the magnitude of your consciousness is to look upon it as a capacity or an accommodation, like a chalice, starting out from the heart center, in the middle of the chest. You don't radiate from the heart center, you simply find room for more and more beings—starting with those beings you find difficult to love and then reaching out farther and farther with the power of the heart—a cosmic emotion beyond human emotion. Sense the compassion of the Mother of the world—the emotion of suffering being transformed into joy. Then awaken to the consciousness of the soul instead of the heart, beyond emotion. You discover the divine perfection in you and watch yourself speeding towards the awareness of divine perfection. Then you realize the One behind all multiplicity, the spaceless behind space, the timeless behind time, the numberless beyond multiplicity, and participate in the great celebrations when all beings converge in the measure of their awareness in the great rejoicing, where they are celebrating the overcoming of limitation and of illusion in the crowning of the King of the universe.*

*Toward the One, the perfection of Love, Harmony, and Beauty, the Only Being, united with all the illuminated souls—you unite yourself with all the illuminated souls—who form the embodiment of the master, the spirit of guidance—all the illuminated souls, whom you reach not only by the power of your thought, but by that great cosmic law of invocation whereby the soul of every creature can find a resonance in the soul of every other creature simply by turning towards him. You stir the hearts of the prophets and the masters and the saints, of all the heavenly beings and all the hierarchies of beings, just by your invocation.*

# CHAPTER 4
# Point Omega

There are many proponents of eastern schools of thought who are now coming to the West and promoting the methods and dogma that were taught many thousands of years ago. An antique has value that new things don't have: the age of a cello, for instance, makes a lot of difference; the wood has matured and the vibrations that have come through it as a result of its being played have transformed the wood. So it is true that the old doctrines and methods, elaborated by very wonderful beings who lived in very special circumstances, have a tremendous value. We must remember that every being stands on the shoulders of those who came before him—just as, in the story of the golem, people stood on one another's shoulders to build a human tower so that the golem could look into the heavens. Still, it doesn't seem to make sense just to follow a method of the past without taking into account what is happening in our time.

What is happening now is exactly what Teilhard de Chardin described: a formation of point omega, which is the integration of all the consciousnesses of men into a unified consciousness. Hazrat Inayat Khan said that you can consider humanity as one being. This is what is called in theology the divine immanence rather than the divine transcendence. Meditation has traditionally, at least in India, been thought of as a way of reaching beyond consciousness of the physical plane to a transcendent, original condition—original not necessarily in time, but *in principio:* the causal plane from which everything descends into manifestation. This was regarded as the ideal of meditation. Then Ramakrishna said, "Can you not meditate with your eyes open? Can you not have samadhi with open eyes?"

This was the beginning of the turning point, and Ramakrishna was the precursor of the New Age. He realized the importance of bringing a sublime consciousness right down into life. Normally, when you're in samadhi you are not aware of what goes on in the physical plane. If a fly crawls on your nose or someone sits in front of you, you are not conscious of it; you are in what I call "alpha consciousness." Alpha consciousness with iota or personal consciousness is samadhi with open eyes, and there are very few beings who have been able to do this—to be in a very high state of consciousness and still be aware of the thinking of other people.

It is very difficult to combine these two vantage points at the same time. I call it "stereoscopic consciousness," which means being conscious on two different levels at the same time. It's like walking with a telescope in one eye and a microscope in the other, and it's very hard to walk that way. But we have, somehow, an extraordinary capacity for integrating levels of consciousness.

For some time, I thought, "This is it! Samadhi with open eyes!" I was so convinced. But then it occurred to me, "Why do you try to look at things from alpha consciousness, which is the original state before incarnation, and then see everything in terms of that? How about the purpose? Isn't that more important than the cause?" Actually, it was the teaching of Hazrat Inayat Khan that led me to see the strangulation of the law—the law that says that if you've done this, you have to suffer that. There's no freedom in it. But the purpose is a freeing from the law.

The creation is continually being reimprovised and renewed, and we are part of it. So our freedom is the expression of the divine freedom against what used to be the divine freedom before it became fossilized in the form of law. Many people think they are contravening the divine law by their freedom, whereas in the real sense of the word, their freedom is the way that the divine freedom manifests through them.

I often think of the genius who is working on DNA structures. I don't know whether he thinks he is working all of this out, but seen from the real perspective, what he is doing is in fact the one and only Consciousness working through this instrument—the scientist—and discovering His own being in the life processes within the cell. We always think of God as another being; if we could only realize that we *are* God. It's not that He is working through us: we *are* Him. It gives you a completely different way of looking at things, because inasmuch as we are God, He is a reality down here and not just up there. That is why the great Sufi Niffari said, "Why do you seek for God up there? He is here, here!" All our meditation was traditionally based on alpha consciousness— up there—whereas what it should be is experiencing the divine consciousness working right down here in manifestation— what I call "omega consciousness" or "omega samadhi."

When this realization was new for me, I thought this was "it," until the thought occurred to me, "Why do you want to exclude alpha samadhi? It's important, too!" So the perfect meditation would be a combination of alpha consciousness, iota consciousness, and omega consciousness: being able to see the cause, being aware of your personal consciousness, and seeing the divine intention working through all things together with the law.

Another thought that has become stronger and more evident is how painful it is for the divine Being to accept limitation so that each part of Himself will be free. Of course, all great beings experience that more intensely than others; they experience the suffocation of the prison not just of the physical body but of the conditions in which we must work when we have to contend with the freedom of other people. People are sometimes rather reckless—and certainly ego-tistical—and sometimes violent and cruel and dishonest. It's a real suffering to deal with all this, and is, I think, what is meant by the Hebrew word *zumzum*: that God has to limit Himself in order to descend.

So in iota—or personal—consciousness, there is a lot of suffering, because of the limitation in which it must allow itself to be circumscribed. And yet, somehow freedom is able to manifest in a way that it couldn't in alpha, just as you sometimes can express yourself more freely within a limited frame than you could if there were no limitations. For example, a horse will run faster with a rider on it if the rider is not too heavy; and while your improvisation on the piano might be fine, you can "say" more if you improvise in a limited structure, as Bach did. Somehow the divine freedom comes through in these limitations.

There is a tendency to think of purpose as being something that is moving towards a state at the end of time. But there's no end to the purpose, so you can never say, "at the end of time"—especially since there is no end of time anyway. But one tends to think of the purpose as being somewhere in the infinite future and to think of the cause as being right back in the past. In fact, you have to think of the cause as happening now, because it's in the eternal present, and of the purpose as already existing now; this is why Hazrat Inayat Khan said that God attains his fulfillment in the being who manifests His perfection on the earth. You don't have to think of it as something that will happen in the future. You have to free your mind from the association of cause with the past and purpose with the future. This is why I prefer to use small alpha rather than capital alpha, and small omega rather than capital omega.

It is true that omega in this sense does develop in the course of time. We can say it's already there because it reaches beyond time; Teilhard de Chardin said omega was already there in alpha. What, then, is omega consciousness? You can't grasp it if you think of it as something towards which we are moving, because it is always moving further. It is in fact our joint consciousness—our collective consciousness. And, more and more, we're beginning to realize ourselves as one being in modern time. Omega is the ability to enter into the consciousness of what seems to be another person and experience what it's like to be that person, and it reaches its fulfillment when you realize that that person is really another yourself.

The omega consciousness evidences itself when seeing another person coming and thinking, "It is I who is coming." The best compliment you could pay a person is to say, "Hello, me!" Hindu gurus often write the salutation, "Dear self." It's so nice to say that: "Dear self." It's like a leaf of a tree writing to another leaf of the same tree and saying "Dear self" because they're all part of the tree.

In the last century there has been a very strong accent on the strife of the individual against other individuals, on competition and on the affirmation of egotism. On the other hand, we might think, "Well, do you mean to say that we should lose our ego? Doesn't ego have a purpose?" Of course it does. The beauty of life is, in the words of Prentice Mulford, "Infinity in a finite fact and eternity in a temporal act." You can think of each individual as a pyramid that has its apex separate from and its base in common with all other bases. When we function in a polarized way, from the apex of the pyramid, then we think of ourselves as a fraction of the totality and of the world as other than ourselves or outside ourselves. But when we function from the vantage point of the base of the pyramid, then we experience ourselves as being the totality. Normally this can happen only when we've lost consciousness of our individuality; that's why al-Hallaj said, "Ana'-l Haqq"—"I am the Truth"—which says that he is God. The Sufis say he said it when he had lost his ego consciousness: it would be the most vulgar ego trip imaginable for anyone to say "I am God" while still conscious of his ego. You can only operate from that vantage point when you have lost the sense of yourself.

The ego is important because it is through the multiplication of egos that the totality has been able to attain the fulfillment that happens on the earth. The reason for that fulfillment is that all that was latent in the original state has been able to cross-pollinate. We are not only the heirs to the whole universe; there is more in us than what we have inherited, and that is a result of our interaction with other beings. It is what Hazrat Inayat Khan called the character, which is made up of acquired characteristics rather than inherited ones. Someone may have had a great influence on your being, and you may have been transformed by your interaction with that being. This wasn't possible before your incarnation through the different spheres; it wasn't possible in the causal state. So something is gained by life on earth, and it is gained through the ego.

We don't, therefore, want to just discard the ego; we want to coordinate it with the impersonal, infinite dimension.

Hazrat Inayat Khan put it very beautifully when he said, "The edges of my own walls began to hurt my elbows." We want the ego to develop a kind of elasticity that will enable it to incorporate the totality. Actually, the curious thing is that you are never so rich a personality as when you are absolutely impersonal. It's strange how all the qualities of the personality come through when you become completely impersonal. When you become free from your personality, then it begins to unfold.

It's all so wonderful that you feel like dancing for joy, discovering the meaningfulness of your life. There really is no excuse to have a long face—it's only caused by getting stuck in one's ego consciousness. The only reason to be sad is on account of the suffering of other beings, not because of your own. And there is a lot of suffering in the world. The point of omega consciousness is that your consciousness extends to the consciousness of all beings, so you're always picking up SOSs from people asking for help.

Most of us are circumscribed in the immediate environment, and it's very confining to be caught up in the immediate environment. That's what iota consciousness is—a confinement of consciousness that is focalized in the sense of being the person you think you are. It's wonderful to be able to extend your consciousness, to infiltrate it into the consciousness of all beings. These are the meditations of the future, and the next step in the process of evolution: collective consciousness. Hazrat Inayat Khan calls it planetary consciousness, which is a wonderful way of putting it. One day we may well have to use that consciousness to deal with beings on other planets. We'll begin to realize our identity as humans. And then we'll be able to reach farther than that to consciousness of the galaxy—and eventually even to universal consciousness.

CHAPTER 5

# From the Solitude of Unknowing
# to the State of Unity

There may be some confusion in the minds, hearts, and souls of quite a few people who are seeking a spiritual path, because there are so many wonderful teachers whose teachings may at first seem rather conflicting unless one can really make a synthesis of them. There is a phenomenon that might be called the paradox of the New Age: literally thousands of seeking people have found their way to the shores of India and gone on what is known as the "guru hunt," only to return disappointed or to adopt some exotic cult that may be even more exacting than the church they left behind—swapping one religion for another, and never getting down to the real thing they were looking for, which was a completely free approach to a genuine spiritual experience.

This is all part of a major development in consciousness — the welding together of all the component parts of humanity into a whole. For this reason, it is sometimes necessary to go a little bit overboard and become more Muslim than the Muslims or more Hindu than the Hindus. It's a part of the process whereby humanity is becoming more conscious of itself as a whole at the level that is the most important of all, which is the spiritual level. This is, of course, happening willy-nilly, and some teachers are horrified to see people chanting Hindu mantrams and then doing Sufi dances, and so forth. The spiritual realm has become a hodgepodge.

Teachers in India are, of course, very traditional, and don't understand how it is possible for people to think they can follow several paths at the same time. Yet the pressure of the current is such that several teachers have been obliged to come to the realization that something is happening on the face of the earth, and that this is the new way, whether we like it or not. It means giving up a lot of frontiers and barriers, and is forcing the teachers themselves to find new ways for themselves.

Sometimes practices are adopted rather superficially, without a real understanding of what they are all about. So, although I do not believe that reason can really carry us very far, we might try to see clearly what this is all about.

On one hand, there seems to be a quest for an experience beyond life—exploring the far reaches of no man's land beyond human consciousness and exploring different forms of perception, such as extrasensory perception. This is the forward march of consciousness as Teilhard de Chardin describes it in *The Phenomenon of Man*, moving and breaking into new horizons and extending beyond the purview of the grasp of consciousness when it is centered in the sense of ego or self.

In fact, we don't even know what consciousness is: it is the greatest mystery there is. As far as we do know, and according to their behavior, atoms and cells, plants, bodies, minds, and possibly something else within us are all endowed with awareness. When the awareness of each cell of the body together with all the others composes one joint awareness, we call it body awareness. At the same time, there is an awareness that is called "mind" in English and *manas* in Sanskrit. There is no word for it in German or French: it is neither *Gemut* nor *esprit*. The reason for this is that the notion of the mind is so remote, and it is really probably true to say that there is no such thing as the mind. We can say that at the mental level there is a kind of consciousness and that there is a conjunction or dovetailing or overlapping between body consciousness and mind consciousness. There are also other levels, of course.

When consciousness operates in a body with a central nervous system, as all sentient bodies have, then, of course, experiences are referred to a center. It is the very organization of the body that builds a center and centers awareness, organizing its sensory input. This is why we can have the thought "I am" or "I am a person": it arises out of the very constitution of the body. This is the way things look when consciousness is centered.

The experience of meditation is the experience of the way things look when consciousness is *not* centered. The whole process that is followed by yoga and the Hindu Vedanta is the destruction of the sense of I-ness. Buddhism, too, works to destroy the I-ness that is apart from another being. When this happens, consciousness gushes with a tremendous force. It breaks through the barriers that have been forced upon it and begins to become aware of reality at a cosmic, breathtaking level. If you are not used to it, this breakthrough can destroy the understanding unless you have tremendous strength, and are sufficiently trained and willing to take in the gradually increasing breadth of horizon that opens up before your perspective—until you reach the condition that is called "illumination," when you can encompass the whole breadth of reality in one take without having your mind blown.

There is a natural protection afforded us against that which we cannot encompass or meet because we do not have the strength of mind or courage to face it. This is simply that kind of blackout that is ignorance. You can reach a point where you are protected by what is called "the cloud of unknowing" —which is, exactly, *maya*. *Maya* is the measure of our ignorance, and at the same time the measure of our protection.

So we can destroy our ego-centered consciousness and find ourselves in the darkness. We are like a child that has just been born, who, when he opens his eyes, doesn't know what he sees; it takes him a lot of time to realize that what he sees makes sense. In meditation, we develop the ability to see sense where we didn't see sense before. We discover a completely new pattern of logic. And then it dawns upon us that our way of experiencing and knowing is very limited—that it is subject to the limitations of ignorance. We realize that we are just like puppets in the hands of all the things that are working upon us, that we simply react to impressions and are not the masters of situations.

Yet we know that one of our noblest qualities is being free, and that we are endowed with some measure of freedom and can conquer more freedom. We feel that the rishi in the Himalayas, the dervish, and the contemplative have explored the domains of freedom—which, of course, they have—and can tell us how to extend our consciousness beyond the limits of ordinary day-to-day consciousness and conduct us beyond it. We know that the price of the experience is a kind of death —the death of our ego, the death of our notion of ourselves and of the otherness of things, among many other notions. But if I overcome the centering of my consciousness, then you are I. That is the meaning of contemplation: there is no distinction between subject and object. This is the knowledge the Upanishads refer to—the knowledge that subject and object are one, so that there is no sense of otherness.

This experience, which is often attributed to God, is the kind of experience we have when the notion of the self has been eliminated, so quite naturally many of us feel that that is meditation: a way of extending consciousness beyond the normal limits. This requires us to give up the vantage point of individual experience and go on what, unfortunately, often does seem much like a trip. Because of this, many people do it for the sake of the experience, and because we have all already had so many experiences, it is possible to reach a point of satiety and feel that this is simply another experience that we can have and that contemplation is the best way to have it.

There are shortcuts like drugs that are illegal and that have a lot of disadvantages; doing it the hard way is the way the rishis do it, and the advantage of that is that it leaves a lasting state of awareness that cannot be lost. It's not like a trip; you don't go up and then down again. Your consciousness remains open.

When you have abandoned the notion of self, consciousness is no longer centered, and at a certain point it becomes omniscient. But, as we noted before, if you force the issue, there is a tendency to lose consciousness altogether. Unless consciousness maintains its continuity without losing itself, you simply get into a trance state where nothing is gained. We want to be able to maintain the Ariadnean thread of memory, to maintain a reference point of consciousness—the focal point on earth.

Practically speaking, in meditation you do remember having thought the way you thought when you were in your ordinary consciousness; you remember having had a body, you believe you may be able to recover the use of it, and you even remember having had a mind. You realize that the way you are thinking now is very different from the way you think in your mind: what you see now is the principle behind the thinking of the mind. You're seeing the general instead of the particular; and when you know the general, the particular is just a matter of application.

Normally, the awareness of the body and the awareness of the mind are partitioned away from the awareness of the higher areas of your being by the cloud of unknowing, because nature believes that you will not be able to face all the degrees of experience at the same time. When we sleep, nature closes off the layers of consciousness at the physical and mental levels and opens another level of consciousness immediately above the normal, logical, mental way of thinking. The nature of reality thus experienced is much broader than that of everyday reality. Your personality is different.

It is possible that we remember our dreams, but do we remember what we felt like in our dreams when we remembered our diurnal consciousness? Generally, the awareness of the memory of diurnal consciousness in your dreams is cut away when you are exposed to your ordinary perception. The reason for this is that our sense of I-ness is so different in the dream consciousness. We are much more courageous—prepared to knock at the door of our boss and ask for a raise—and we can do things like flying, which we actually feel in our physical bodies. We are conscious of a wider degree of possibilities in our dream consciousness. This is what the contemplative is aware of.

In dreams, we discover a richness to our being that we didn't know we had. And as we forget the richness when we come back down into diurnal consciousness, we generally return back to our limited personalities. But if you are able to remember what you really are when you are in your diurnal consciousness, then you will be it. And that is the secret of meditation. It is not just an experience; it enables you to unfold your being. The secret is to keep the door open between the mental plane and what is called the plane of dreams.

You know that you can be suspended between dream

consciousness and awakened consciousness. In this state, if you just shift a little bit in one direction, the door will close to dream consciousness and you will go right into diurnal consciousness; if you shift a little bit in the other direction, the doors to diurnal consciousness will close and you will go right into dream consciousness. But if you can keep yourself steady on that threshold—and it is rather difficult—you keep the door open. Then the impressions of your dream state are brought through to your physical or diurnal consciousness.

This is what we try to do in meditation. While the center of consciousness dissolves, there is a memory of having had a body; in fact, there is still a feeling of a body down there. You don't think anymore that it is your body; there is just a sense of bodiness. In fact, one of the ways of destroying the center of consciousness that gives you your personal awareness is to envision your body as part of the totality of bodies instead of envisioning it as your self. In Buddhism, for example, you look at your body as a sequence in a series of bodies, one engendering the other; you are aware of the bodies of your parents and ancestors. If you see the whole thing dynamically, there is no such thing as your body—it's just a series of bodies following one another. And once you realize that, the sense of yourself as a body will disappear. In this high state of consciousness, you only remember that there is a state of bodiness down there that has certain advantages, but quite a lot of disadvantages; and unless you autosuggest yourself to return, it can be very difficult to do so. If you go very high, it's difficult to come down. You don't see the point anyway.

The same thing applies to the mind, although it is more subtle. Everyone will say that what holds people back in meditation is that thoughts seem to force their way over the threshold between the conscious and unconscious mind. You're subjected to these thoughts, and you think, "How can I still the mind?" The solution is very simple: the key to what is called "mind control" is not in the will. What is called "will" is the will of the conscious mind, whereas there is also a will of the unconscious. The will of the conscious mind cannot tackle the forces of the unconscious, so you have to train the will of the unconscious by your conscious will, and then your unconscious will takes over. For example, when you are learning to play the piano or to type, you must first learn the motion by your conscious will, and then the unconscious will takes over—and does it much better than you could do with your conscious will. Once the unconscious has taken over, if you try to intervene with your conscious will you spoil the whole thing. You just have to let the automatic action take over.

So in meditation, the only way to tackle the very disturbing impressions of the mind that are knocking at the door because they want attention—and, as Buddha showed, it is these very thoughts that draw us into incarnation—is by an attitude of total detachment and indifference. In taking this attitude, however, we must remember that detachment is always the counterpart of something positive. We must not think of it as a negative thing. The positive counterpart of detachment is ecstasy: detachment without ecstasy takes you into the void.

When we are tired, of course, we seek peace. Somewhere in the depths of our being, there is a feeling that there is something there in peace that is of great value. We don't always have the force to find it ourselves; we count on Christ or the church or a guru to do it for us. But the important thing is that we have within us this tremendous aspiration for an emotion that is beyond emotions, which is no emotion: serenity and peace. The Sufis put this in a very beautiful way: they call it sharing the nostalgia of God for returning to His state of unknowing.

There seem to be two movements in the inbreath and outbreath of God. The outbreath is the motion towards manifestation, which the Sufis call delivering the latencies within His being from the solitude of unknowing. In the return, God resorbs multiplicity into the solitude, which is a state of unity. We experience the same thing in ourselves— although, more accurately, we should say that God experiences this through us, or we experience it through Him: being carried into the sense of oneness, which is a rest from multiplicity.

There are also two attitudes of the soul experienced by the Sufis: turning towards the orient, from which one's light comes, and seeking oneself in another oneself; and turning toward the occident, which is the world of shadow, and seeking in forms that which one has not been able to discern in the formless. There is something in us that seeks the world of forms and experiences through the senses, the mind, and all the vehicles that have been given to us. But then there comes a moment when we seek the reverse and, as the Sufis say, we are participating in the act whereby God draws away from multiplicity into unity. This is very easily understood, and, unfortunately, many people believe that this is meditation; but it is only one half of meditation. The other half—which completes it—is, as Hazrat Inayat Khan said, to "make God a reality."

The longing for freedom and peace could lead you to flee your environment, leave society behind, give up action, and go to live in a cell somewhere and spend the rest of your life meditating—and go farther and farther away from physical and mental experience. You reach a point where you remember having been; you are not anymore. You cannot even know that you are not, because you're not there to know it. Yet there is a tremendously incisive perception of meaning such as you couldn't possibly see when you were involved in the wheels and mechanisms of existence.

We so often knock our heads against the wall, against fate,

and ask, "Why has fate been so unfair to me?" And when someone we love has died, we say, "No, no!" We cannot accept it; we cannot accept the unacceptable. So the great lesson is to realize *why:* Why did this person die? Why did I fail? Why is life so unfair? At this level of meditation, you see why—but, as we said, you aren't there to see it. But then you have the curious experience of returning from that state and beginning to be aware that you hadn't *been*; you are emerging out of non-being into being, and then remembering that you are the same being that you were before you ceased to be. If you follow this pursuit further—because this is still only half the way—you can traverse the levels described in Hinduism until you reach the absolute and experience *atman,* the one soul. The Buddha himself did not feel that we could ever outline an end, however, and so he always presented us with an endless horizon: the farther you advance, the farther the horizon recedes. So at no time in meditation can you say, "This is it."

# CHAPTER 6

# Meditation

People often say to me, "Please tell me how to meditate; what must I do?" I would say there is a question preliminary to that, and it is, "Why meditate?" We all know there are moments when we seem to attain the zenith of our being—moments when we seem to feel the heartbeat of life. We experience a breakthrough of the forces of joy; there is an awakening, a tremendous awareness, and we seem to be attuned to a very high pitch. We become highly sensitive to a deeper reality. It is quite a contrast to those moments when we have lost this divine touch and are very poor and flat indeed. In all sensitive people there is a tremendous need for unfoldment. We know that we do unfold ourselves in our relationship with reality in the course of communication, and that our experience is generally extremely limiting when it is reduced to experience on the purely physical or mental plane—when it has to pass through the focal center of consciousness that is working at the level of the ego. Some people suffer from frustration, boredom, and even despair because of failure to achieve their purpose. We know that meditation will add many dimensions to our life and experience, for our ordinary experience is composed of about ten percent of what we experience in the totality in meditation. We know that we should be able to experience this reality, these added dimensions, without meditation in the course of everyday life, yet we do not, because it is very difficult: as long as the sun is shining, you cannot see the stars. The subtle reality that is experienced during meditation seems to be blotted out when our senses are full of the more blatant impressions of the outside world. That which is experienced in meditation is very fine and subtle and difficult to sense. Meditation is a special condition in which we are protected from the gross impressions—which come from the same source as the finer impressions, because there is only one source, and that is divine reality in its totality.

There are heritages in us from all different sources, and these are what we experience when we relate to the universe. There is always a confrontation between that which comes from our past and that which is latent within us and springs to life in contact with its counterpart outside. Sometimes the inheritance from the body comes to the fore, at other times the inheritance from previous incarnations or other sources; and sometimes the divine inheritance suddenly transpires, and we become transfigured by the tremendous significance of what comes through us. In meditation we become similar to the impressions we are receiving, just as we become like the impressions we receive on the earth plane. If we live in a gangster world we become gangsters; we receive those impressions and behave like gangsters. In meditation, we bring ourselves into contact with heavenly influences.

How do we proceed? The impressions coming from the senses and from the mind have a confining effect. They are not bad, they are beautiful, but we must understand that we see only as much in nature as there is in our soul—and there are some who cannot see any beauty at all. We must also know that, as Saint John of the Cross said, in comparison with the beauty of God, the beauty of created things is nothing. So in meditation there is movement of the soul towards an object of great beauty that we are able to sense without the senses, and which produces beauty in our being. We might say you have it in you, but until that which is in you is able to express itself, to manifest itself, to unfold itself, it is necessary to capture on the outside the counterpart of that which is inside you.

How can we capture something that does not have physical consistency if it is not captured through the senses? This is not a description of anything that can be experienced in nature. It is possible that the beauty of nature could inspire one to the heights of realization, but that which is captured here is of a different order altogether; nature is only one of the media through which the total divine perfection manifests. Its image is very beautiful, but it is rather limited, because when we think of nature we think of the physical level. There is such a thing as the non-physical level: the level of the divine attributes that manifest through nature but are of a different order from anything that has form and structure in time.

What, then, do we capture? We capture a reality that does not have form and which at first seems to be made up of attributes. But when we proceed further we realize what we are capturing is beyond attributes and that there are several levels of that which we capture. The whole point in meditation is the confrontation with an ineffable something that is being experienced, and in order to experience it we have to be able to listen very attentively; it is like listening to a voice in outer space, or seeing something that is hardly visible. It requires a particular refinement of our awareness, which contrasts with the awareness we have of the denser outer things. It is like being able to perceive things that are less and less concrete or physical, while at the same time using a medium of perfection, which is the level of consciousness that is increasingly enhanced and heightened.

We start with the consciousness of the physical body and leave the objects we perceive outside ourselves, and we try to experience something much more subtle than that which comes through the senses. In order to do this, that which experiences must be something other than the ego consciousness. This is why most people find it difficult to meditate—because they remain in the egoic consciousness. It is the ego consciousness that thinks and decides and feels and perceives, and so long as you maintain your consciousness in that point, there is no meditation, except insofar as the ego consciousness can extend its range upwards. It is elastic, in a way, and can therefore perceive things at the fringe of the field of consciousness that are very subtle. A sensitive person who is anchored on the earth but has fine feelings of perception and intuition will experience even finer feelings of delicacy. But this is not meditation, because meditation is a total transformation of one's whole being, so that suddenly one's awareness is lighted up tremendously, and everything becomes intensely clear: it is an awakening. You have a feeling of having been all this time in darkness; you have been captured by the illusion, and suddenly through meditation you are freed from it. And whereas the kind of joy that has been experienced by the egoic consciousness can be very great indeed—because the egoic consciousness is capable of enjoying beauty, and joy is always connected with beauty—in comparison with the tremendous joy of the awakening consciousness this joy is nothing at all. So the problem is how to transfer your consciousness from the lower center of the ego to this higher consciousness. I have often used the word "egolessness," and also the word "detachment." Hazrat Inayat Khan said, "Indifference and independence are the two wings which enable the soul to fly." Indifference means remaining detached from what is happening, that is, not being personally involved in one's feelings, and independence means not depending upon outer circumstances for one's joy.

We can understand these attitudes of the soul by contrasting them to their opposites. Dependence, for example, is the terrible feeling we have when we depend upon a thing or a person that lets us down. The person who must smoke because it is a habit, or take drugs, or go to the pictures, or have a social life, or whatever, is in a state of dependence. Detachment is the opposite of attachment. We attach ourselves to people and to circumstances. The attainment of the zenith of our being comes at the moment when we have overcome conditioning and coercion. So the first lesson to learn in meditation is to become free inside. It is not possible to meditate unless we disinvolve ourselves emotionally from all things that bind us, and this must be done consciously. It can be a preparatory period before we start meditation. We make an inventory of our lives—how we stand in life, what we want and what we need, how deeply we are involved, how free we are, and how dependent we make others upon us. Are we capable of loving and at the same time freeing the person we love? This is the basic condition for meditation: to become aware of our freedom. Then when we begin to meditate and a thought comes, we may be sure that the thought is always due to our involvement with whatever the thought expresses. The thought is simply the messenger to tell you that you are bound by something. It is always based upon emotional involvement. This does not mean that you should not involve yourself emotionally, but if you wish to follow this path—this royal road—you must be able to introduce the dimension of freedom into your involvement. Then the world grabs control of you with a vengeance, because you have tried to free yourself from its grasp, and it works through the detours of the unconscious. The thoughts shoot up from the unconscious over the threshold between the unconscious and the conscious into the conscious field.

So long as consciousness is centered in the egoic consciousness it will be aware of these thoughts, because, as Martin Buber said, every "I" presupposes either an "It" or a "Thou." So the "I" of the ego consciousness presupposes an "It"—an object—and consequently thoughts will crop up when your consciousness is centered in the ego. The only way to free yourself from the tyranny of thoughts is to rise above the consciousness of the ego.

The secret of lifting consciousness to the next level is to be able to relate to the "Thou" instead of the "It." Instead of relating to the objective world, you relate to a presence. This is a magic word and a key word: the divine presence. What is the difference between the presence and the object? The object has a form, a quality. The presence does not have a form or quality; it is not localized in space. Something else in you is aware of the presence than that which is aware of the object. And that is why meditation is so closely related with religion: whether we like it or not, it is an experience of God and not an experience of the objectivized form of God in the universe.

Only the longing of the soul for communion with the principle of itself will enable us to jump the barrier between the egoic consciousness and the higher form of consciousness. We turn either toward the orient or toward the occident. We turn toward the occident in order to see the face of God as it is manifested in the form. We turn toward the orient to meet the principle of which we are the image, and then we are no longer the subject. The principle is the subject of which we are the image. We seek for the image of God in the forms in the west—the world of exile—but in meditation we orient ourselves towards the source from which our consciousness comes. Therefore we cannot acquire consciousness or look upon the source of our consciousness; we can only turn toward it, as the sunflower turns toward the sun. We are trying to capture something from outer space that is embodied in us. We are not trying to observe something. It is because in meditation so many people wish to *observe* that they fail in meditation. If you observe something you must humiliate it: you make it the object of your knowledge. The right relationship with a person is to share or commune rather than to observe. In this way, you are seeing yourself in him while he sees himself in you.

Now we have two secrets that we can make use of in meditating. The first one is that you go on a journey and you leave something behind. You leave the objective world of exile behind you. You know that you will return, but for the moment you leave it behind you; you want to be free, because you are following the aspiration of your soul, to which you generally do not give access. People are very hard on their souls. For once, let your soul have its way. Your soul is like a mirror. It is turned toward the world and filled with the impressions of the world, and it espouses the contour of the forms of the world; it becomes the world, but when it turns the other way all the impressions are gone in one second. The soul is as pure as the mirror; it is never stained. It can in one moment free itself. Meditation is the turning of the soul, withdrawing its attention from the hold of the world.

When the soul turns inward it is free, and we know what an attitude of freedom means—it is like walking in the high mountains and leaving the cities behind. The attitude should be, "It does not matter," which is precisely the opposite of the attitude you adopt in life when you have to assume responsibility. Meditation is only for a period of time, which must be short. I propose a half-hour in the morning and a half-hour in the evening; after that one must return to the life of responsibility. What we want to avoid is wandering, being suspended between two worlds: not being completely in a state of meditation and not being completely active in life. It is like sitting on the fence. We want to become active, efficient workers in the evolution of the planet Earth, fully conscious of our responsibilities, of our duties, of our involvement—but with a plus, which is those extra dimensions you can get in meditation together with the sovereignty that comes with detachment, the insight and awareness that come from the awakening of consciousness, and the illumination and the power that come from egolessness. Those are the qualities we find in everyday life, and we know we can find them beyond life. So we are either completely active or deeply imbued with the meditative state. But meditation is no daydream and it is not laziness. On the contrary, it is a very active thing, only a different direction of activity than that which goes on in life. You now walk, sit, and speak, as Buddha says, with style. Meditation is not relaxation. It is very intense.

So our first secret is detachment; that is, we adopt exactly the opposite of the attitude we adopt in active life and say, "It does not matter." For the moment the only thing that matters is the confrontation between the soul and perfection. In other words, you are looking into the sun, and what happens on the earth is unimportant. What matters is what you receive from the sun. If you adopt this attitude uncompromisingly, no thought can possibly bother you, because it is all unimportant. This is not an attitude of the will, it is an attitude of the soul. There is a tremendous joy, and the ordinary thoughts have no importance at all. Meditation must be a total commitment at that moment of communion.

The second secret is a transfer of the focal center of our consciousness from the ego center to the higher center, which does not experience "I-ness" anymore, but only "Thou-ness." This can only be achieved by a tremendous attention, a total commitment—nothing else matters for this moment. This is the time when you are coming into contact with something very subtle, throwing the arrow at a very great distance to the bull's eye. As the Zen archer says, the arrow is already in the target before you shoot it, because here you transcend the realm of causality. Where there are thoughts there is causality, for one thought leads to another. But at this level, time does not have any part to play. Time has a part to play where there is space—where you are concerned with structures and images. Time is a dimension not accounted for in space; where there is no more image there is no time relationship and, consequently, no causality. Therefore, there is no bondage and no conditioning, only freedom.

Before you reach this point there are intermediary points. You may have visions—for example, the faces of angels or temples of light, or of cataclysms or people who have passed to the other side. You may also have audition, hearing sounds such as the symphony of the spheres. These are only intermediary stages that you should not allow to bind or hold. You should not encourage this state of affairs because it has the effect of swelling the ego, and when you return to ordinary consciousness there is a temptation to boast about the experiences, which centers the consciousness in the ego. You might even re-interpret the vision incorrectly. It is not advised to discuss these experiences. Meditation is not an experience, it is a communion; where there is experience there is an "I" and an "It," and one who speaks about a vision is in an intermediary stage. There is still an "It," although it is a transfigured "It." One can be stuck on all or any of these levels, such as the astral, and many describe this state. There is a division of consciousness. Psychologically it corresponds to schizophrenia: one assumes two personalities. One set of experiences relates to one part of consciousness and another set relates to another, and thus one is split between two things, so astral travel presents some danger. It will often manifest itself in schizophrenia in the person concerned.

Many people are not capable of coping with these two forms of consciousness, because they have not been integrated. Meditation is really integrating the various levels of consciousness into a unit; by extending the awareness in high levels and then always relating the experience in the high levels to the experience in the lower levels, you are able to build up a harmonious whole. It is a very tempting and very dangerous experience, for you may not be able to cope with the onslaught of the astral beings that you contact, and you can come completely under their influence and be subjugated by them. Many people have done this and found themselves unable to free themselves from these astral beings. This is just a warning. The intermediary steps are wonderful, they are beautiful; let us take them as they come, and go beyond. Saint Theresa of Avila says you will start seeing such beautiful lights and hearing such beautiful sounds—you might even receive messages—and it is so wonderful you will want them repeated again and again. But the time comes when you must cease wanting to experience them.

What, then, *is* meditation? It is a tremendous breakthrough of the forces of glorification. I use the word jubilation. Meditation attains its fullness when it becomes a hosanna, a hallelujah, and that is not a personal joy, which is why I say jubilation instead of joy. The forces of joy can become hysterical when they are personal, whereas soul light, because it is egoless, is sublime. It corresponds to the passage from fire to light. We can distinguish between the joy of Brahms when in his symphony he overcomes the shadows of despair, which is a personal joy in the soul, and the jubilation of Bach, which is beyond all things. Bach expresses the motion of the planets and the harmony of the spheres, which represent a higher order of joy than personal joy—a joy of cosmic dimensions. This joy is more intense; it can be breathtaking, like the hosannas of the High Mass of Bach. It is beyond the personal.

In meditation we are attuning ourselves. All the values of our being are being adjusted and attuned to a higher pitch. If I may use a mixed metaphor, we have to purify the organ in order to be able to attune it. We have to make it egoless, because the ego cannot cope with joy. It appropriates joy to itself, whereas in meditation we become like an Aeolian harp that responds to the winds of the heavens and brings a symphony through itself. Meditation is essentially art, only the object of this art is not outside: it is oneself. We muster all the forces and all the elements within ourselves. We are compounded of so many things: there is strength in us, there is joy, there is peace, there is understanding, and there is balance. All of these elements are integrated and brought into a whole. They become part of our awareness; instead of being objects they become live parts of ourselves. We only achieve this by letting something greater than our will and our consciousness take over.

Then something happens in our consciousness. For example, we do not feel the outline of the body. There is a kinesthetic feeling of not being our body anymore. Also, we are not functioning in the mind, so we do not identify with the mind. In fact, the mind seems to be rather insignificant at this point. We do not go out of our mind—we know that we can always take out of it as much as we put in. It is within our reach; we can use it; but we have to transcend it.

Now we have carried consciousness beyond the point where it is the consciousness of a limited being, and we allow consciousness to function beyond the limitations of the body and the mind. At that moment we do not think of ourselves as a limited consciousness. We are aware simply of consciousness, total consciousness, which seems to illuminate everything it penetrates. This corresponds to a feeling of transparency: we do not offer resistance to consciousness.

From the moment that we do not appropriate consciousness, it extends beyond all space and begins to flow through us, and we feel as though every cell of the body were being illuminated by consciousness. It is a feeling that corresponds to illumination. You can imagine the Buddha sitting under the bodhi tree and being completely light, as though he were penetrated through and through with light. Even the brain seems to be penetrated with light, and then we identify ourselves with this luminous consciousness—we have become a luminous consciousness—and everything has become clear. This is what I call the awakening. By that time we feel in communication with a tremendous reality that does not have to manifest itself in matter to be: it simply is. That everything manifests itself in matter is only an expression of this reality.

This is the point at which Hazrat Inayat Khan tells us to commune with the hierarchy of the government of the world: the masters, saints, and prophets. This will give us a sense of our responsibility upon the earth. Otherwise we would be inclined to lose ourselves in the tremendous reality we are experiencing. This is the moment to turn back again. For each one of us, there is a moment to turn back. Do not go beyond this moment. As soon as you reach that point, turn back again, and know how to turn back. Do not come back from meditation with a bang.

There are four directions in meditation. One is from the outside towards within, and that is detachment. The second is from within upwards, and that is independence. The third is from upwards downwards, and that is incarnation. The fourth comes from inwards outward, and that is radiation. So the second half of meditation, after we have attained the zenith of our being (which is indescribable in words), is to return back down again—or, rather, to bring all we have experienced down and embody it and radiate it. At the moment when we have attained the zenith there is a brief loss of contact with the earth plane. We try to reduce this moment, and, in fact, we can only experience it as we inhale, at the moment when the breath is retained. In the more advanced forms of meditation there is a time when the contact with the earth plane is reduced to a minimum and becomes like the memory of something that is very unreal, although you know how to go back there again. We, too, having reached this stage, know the way back again. I did know a lady who was practicing *kundalini* yoga, the awakening of the dormant energy at the base of the spine, who lost consciousness for three days and could not come back; and even then it took weeks and weeks before she was completely back again. I do not want to frighten you, but there are reasons why we must be so careful. When we are doing these things we have to know how to proceed correctly. The preparation gives us a very definite and concrete method to follow. Then we launch ourselves into meditation. Continually measure your strength and go back again, and then next time you can go a little farther. Always be the master of the situation.

At every stage on your ascent you must also know how to descend. Beware of the two forces that are continually acting upon you: the forces of buoyancy and the forces of gravity. The force of gravity can be felt on the body, and has a pull on every part of our being, including our soul. That is why we are incarnated—because this gravity has a pull on us and the pull increases when one is near the Earth. You can maintain some part of your being within the gravitational area, and that part of your being will pull the rest of your being back down again. The only thing that will do this is a sense of responsibility, because the thing that holds you back in meditation is your earthiness, and if you free yourself of this, what is going to bring you back? Nothing; you will want to stay up there. It is very painful to have to come back after all one experiences there. The only thing that can bring you back is your feeling of responsibility, which is your feeling of love for other people, because they need you, and that is what you feel when you are up there. You say, "Yes, I must return because I have things to do." And so you return.

We hope that meditation will not make people feel less inclined to face their responsibilities. We hope, on the contrary, that it will make people more aware of their responsibilities. It would be too bad to come down and not bring something down with you. In fact, the whole purpose of going up there was not to learn how to stay there, but to be better able to meet your responsibilities. Hazrat Inayat Khan used the word "domain" or "kingdom." Each one of you is a king or a queen in your own right, and the domain in which you serve is the domain of your influence upon other human beings. We wish to become more capable, so we wish to come back better persons. We wish to come back radiant, highly sensitive, peaceful, and sovereign, and so we bring a power down—a form of energy that is quite different from the energy that propelled us upwards. It is very potent; we are baffled by it; we are completely overwhelmed by its strength and beauty. The best word for it is "sovereignty," because it imposes respect. It is nobility and peacefulness, it is silence; it has a celestial nature. One has a feeling of having been entrusted with something very holy and celestial. Mercury, the messenger of the gods, has the duty of communicating this beautiful thing. And you do not need to work for it—the less you do about it, the better. It just *is*. It radiates its own light. Then you have to be able to play the game, and not allow that which has been experienced to be appropriated by the ego. The ego is essentially something that appropriates things. It wants to possess things, and it will want to possess that power too. So we might consider ourselves to be very important people, and have a very holy face. We have to recover the human touch, and that is where egolessness is so important.

It is a time to be a child amongst children and to be as unimportant and natural; it is a time to screen other people from the intensity of the light, because it might be too strong. It can completely unbalance a person.

You must come down very slowly and gradually and be conscious that the only way for your lower self to be able to cope with the light you have received from above is to radiate that energy as it comes down. Don't hold it. This is the moment of the vow or the consecration commitment—the moment when you renew your covenant with the masters, saints, and prophets to serve them. In this way we help them to impose order, by assuming it in our own actions. You have to act according to the standard you have reached. On your descent, you will find that by having ascended you will have opened doors to the heavenly spheres. You will have drawn the attention of angelic beings who rejoice as soon as someone moves upward. There is a tremendous rejoicing in the heavens. These beings were described in the accounts of Buddha's and Jesus' descents through the different spheres. This happens to every person who lifts his consciousness even a little way. There is an immediate response—a jubilation—and you are the center of this jubilation and rejoicing; and as you come down you may be aware of these beings. They give you their blessing, and the moment of receiving this blessing in great humility is the moment of the covenant; and then you come down.

## MEDITATION PRACTICE

*First, relax the muscles of the back, the spinal cord, the arms, and the legs. Then sit in a very upright position, the spinal cord absolutely straight. If you sit on a book or cushion, that is best, for then your knees are on the ground. If once you have done this, you will realize how very comfortable it is. It forces the spine to be straight. Otherwise the knees are a little too high, and the spinal cord is not straight. Now you are ready for the takeoff. You leave everything behind, and assume an attitude of total detachment. You do not give up the impressions from the outside world—that is, the perception—you leave the mind behind. Then you give up your physical or egoic consciousness. Tune your soul to a very fine pitch. Now give up the frontiers of your being, whether they are the physical body or the mind, and imagine the tremendous richness that flows through you and that is you. Imagine that you are the incorporation of the whole universe. You are continually capturing elements out of space. You begin to assume cosmic dimensions.*

*Now let cosmic consciousness flow through you without appropriating it; you experience an awareness of cosmic consciousness—consciousness frees itself from its support. This is the time to launch yourself upwards: identify yourself with pure, luminous consciousness. You become totally transparent, and the consciousness is egoless. At this point, you feel the pull of the gravity of the earth and you also feel the buoyancy of the soul. The farther the buoyancy of the soul draws you upwards, the more you become aware of the jubilation and glorification of the higher spheres. It is sublime; you cannot experience it from your egoic consciousness. Your consciousness must be freed from that center. You have lifted yourself beyond the realm of thought. The next thing to do is to glorify yourself—partake in the glorification. Raise your consciousness and attune yourself to the highest point, where your whole being becomes an act of glorification. You experience the peace of this high altitude; you seem to feel a tremendous power—a very subtle and sublime power. You are now imbued with this power.*

*Now you redirect your consciousness downward, and bring*

*down your vision of beauty and your sense of peace and the very subtle power of the higher planes—the nobility and the sovereignty—and radiate it as you move downward. You feel a rejoicing of the planes through which you have passed, and you feel committed to manifest that which you have experienced. The moment of the blessing descends upon you—the moment to renew the covenant and link yourself with the masters, saints, and prophets of the great hierarchy of the government of the world, united with all the illuminated souls who form the embodiment of the master, the spirit of guidance. You feel the influence of the higher spheres still working around you; you are carrying the atmosphere of the higher spheres with you, and it is as though you were entrusted with something very sacred.*

*You can always recapture your contact with the higher planes. Bring your consciousness down by allowing the pull of responsibility—the feeling that you have something to do and accomplish—to draw you back. Maintain that state of awakening, of acute awareness, of high-powered sensitivity— the power of the divine beings, the peace, and the sovereignty —but do not lose the common touch. A channel has been opened up, and once it has been cleared you can always establish communication upwards at any time. Keep the line of communication open.*

CHAPTER 7

# New Dimensions
# of Consciousness

There is a relationship between realization and our unfoldment: we unfold in the measure of our ability to understand what's happening in the universe. We have been invited to see into the mind of the universe. We are participating in our bodies in the nature of the fabric of the planet, which is part of the planetary system and of the whole physical universe; and at the same time we are able to look into and see the meaning behind it to some extent, in accordance with the measure of our ability to rise beyond the limits of our individual understanding. This is why people are searching for something beyond their understanding—because they realize, perhaps unconsciously, that our way of explaining things to ourselves is limited by our vantage point.

The idea we have of the physical universe is really a very far cry from the physical universe. We see only one-fiftieth of the frequencies of the electromagnetic spectrum—a slim fraction of the universe. What we see is our impressions of the universe. Do we realize, for example, that the reason we think space is three-dimensional is simply because of the limitation of our brain? Space is multi-dimensional. If you were a two-dimensional animal, for you the world would be like a sheet of paper. It could be curved, but it would still be a sheet of paper, and you would experience only that which intersected the piece of paper. Anything beyond that you wouldn't know, and of what did intersect, you would know only the part that intersected and would be unaware of the rest. In the same way, all that we as beings capable of conceiving of three dimensions experience is that part of the infinitely dimensional universe that is able to come through our three-dimensional sense of reality.

What is much more serious is the idea we have of ourselves, which is totally wrong. Most of us assume that we are our personalities. Some of us assume that we are our bodies, and we let this slip out surreptitiously when we say, "I have a toothache," or, "I have a headache." Ramana Maharshi said, "The body is in pain"—not "*My* body is in pain," but, "*The* body is in pain."

Reaching beyond the personal vantage point is what meditation is all about. What I am trying to do, in any case, is to introduce the way of the ascetic into the middle of life. This is a great challenge—but just imagine that you were endowed with the freedom of the ascetic, so that if your whole world broke down, it wouldn't matter. You would laugh. And you could look upon your body with such detachment that you wouldn't be afraid of death at all.

Imagine being so disciplined that you could perform some of the feats of the ascetic. I made a retreat at the source of the Ganges. The contrast between the heat in Delhi, which is like an oven, and the extreme cold at the source of the Ganges is extraordinary; and there I was, sitting at three in the morning with ascetics. I realized that there was no point in trying to make a fire: it didn't really help, because it didn't make any difference. You just have to love the cold, to delight in it and let all the fresh air come right into your pores. It was extraordinary how I was able to adapt myself to the circumstances. That is the way of the ascetic; after you've done that, you feel there's nothing you can't do. It gives you a wonderful sense of self-confidence. This is something that is very important for people living a kind of artificial life in an affluent society.

We would like to be so full of joy that we're dancing with joy. People tend to wonder if there's something wrong with us if we're dancing with joy, but let's do it all the same. You mustn't force yourself to be full of joy; the objective is to overcome all those arguments you make to yourself against being full of joy—and, of course, there's always a reason.

I visited Mother Teresa in Calcutta, where she and the sisters of her order are looking after the dying. The conditions are just appalling—one can have no idea of what they're putting up with—and they're just full of joy. There is never an excuse not to be full of joy. I've seen people who have survived concentration camps and have been through the most terrible agony; some of them, who were heroic, were just full of joy, and their joy saved other people and gave them the courage to live. There is, in the south of France, a statue of Christ that shows him dancing on the cross—a wonderful symbol of resurrection.

We also want to be free—so free that people can insult us and it doesn't matter; free from our image of our person, so that we don't identify ourselves with our person. Another very challenging thing to be free of is our opinions. Opinion is the result of vantage point. If opinions were right, everyone would agree. You would have to see things from all angles at the same time to see them correctly. Opinion is a stilting thing—like an autopsy or the sum of an experience that has become fossilized. When reality is experienced, it is always new and always alive—and it is something that you can never say.

We also need to be free from personal emotions—the kind of thing you experience when your boyfriend or girlfriend leaves and your whole world collapses. If you are totally free inside, you can love without depending on being loved. The way to do this is to get into the emotion of the cosmos behind the emotion of the individual. Then you realize that you've been invited to the great celebrations in the heavens, and here you are worrying over a little tempest in a teacup. Just imagine how wonderful it is to awaken from your perspective and realize the miracle of life that we're just missing all the time!

How can one tune in to the cosmic dimension? We can start with simple things like walking in the forest. Many of us have the ability to communicate with nature—and, fortunately, there is a whole movement in America now to get back to Mother Earth and understand her and really get into the feeling of communication with the earth. (This has its application in diet as well, and the proof of it will be found in your health eventually.)

So you can learn how to get into the consciousness of the trees and the consciousness of the flowers. What is it like to be a flower? You can know what it's like—all you have to do is sit in front of the flower and just get into the consciousness of that flower. You don't know a flower if you have just looked at it from the outside. Just imagine what it's like to be a flower: just imagine the nostalgia of the flower trying to manifest all the hidden richness of its being, feeling so precarious with such a gentle foothold on the earth, and surviving death by becoming perfume. There is much more in the consciousness of the flower than you could ever experience if you just looked at it from your own vantage point.

Have you ever gotten into the consciousness of your dog? Your dog's main problem is that you treat him like a dog. If you could get into his consciousness, you would realize that he is trying to get into your consciousness all the time, while you are rejecting him and treating him like a dog. He's amazed at your intelligence. He just keeps getting caught up in his instincts, so he can't quite live up to his effort at trying to get into your consciousness. But what a difference there is when *you* try to get into the consciousness of beings!

You can get into the consciousness of human beings, of course. For instance, the person who is making your life impossible: if you start trying to get into his skin, perhaps you'll understand him much better and realize that at least he justifies to himself what he is doing—although whether his justification is right or not, or whether you agree with his arguments, is another question. Or, when you are talking with people, you can, instead of judging them from your personal point of view, be conscious of how you look to them—even how you look physically to them—and of what you are doing to them, instead of just experiencing what they do to you. You get into their consciousness, and then you realize that there is not one being in the universe you can't get in touch with. When you get into the consciousness of all beings, nature assumes a richness you never thought of before. Before, you were just experiencing it from one vantage point; now imagine the richness you experience when walking in nature and getting into the consciousness of all the blades of grass and all the flowers and trees. It gives you a totally different way of looking at the universe: you think of yourself as being looked upon, instead of the one who looks. The whole of nature is totally transfigured. What the Sufi says is that you are experiencing "that which transpires behind that which appears."

At a certain stage in meditation, one begins to sense a kind of programming behind events. But this programming is a kind of ongoing adaptable program, not the kind of thing that is preordained and set from the beginning of time. It takes into account the free will of people. To come back to the person who has been bugging you: he may have been chosen to be the stick with which God nudged you. He may be particularly well adapted to that role, but that's his business. As far as you are concerned, there's some reason why that person was chosen. The Programmer is trying to bring you to a certain realization, and it didn't go the easy way, so it has to go the difficult way—although it doesn't always work even then.

But this glimpse into the programming of the universe is the first dimension of meditation—the cosmic dimension. It is the first way in which you are able to get out of your vantage point: by getting into the vantage point of another. We assume that we can't do it and that we have to see things from our vantage point, because this is the way we have been brought up. We assume that our consciousness is just like a little man inside a machine and that it's right here in the physical body.

The fact is that your consciousness can travel in space. For example, just imagine a pyramid or a tetrahedron in plastic or crystal suspended from the ceiling. You could imagine what it looks like from one angle or another, from above or below. This shows that you can travel your consciousness in space— your consciousness is not restricted to the physical body. The cosmic dimension is reached through the ability to extend your consciousness beyond its focalization. One could say that the total consciousness of the universe is focalized in people, exactly as water is focalized in the eddies in an ocean. What we assume is consciousness is only the way consciousness is focalized. If you study psychophysiology, you find that in the human being, consciousness is both focalized and holistic, which means that consciousness is lenslike: a lens reduces the landscape into an image. So your consciousness reduces the totality of what you experience into something very limited.

On the other hand, our two eyes see totally different pictures and yet make something whole out of those two pictures, so we know that our consciousness can function holistically. You can shift the focus of consciousness to make it act in a more holistic manner: consciousness can extend so that you experience what it is like to be all things. This is the most elementary of all mystical experiences.

Actually, it is very helpful in meditation to realize that only the particle-like aspect of our body is localized in space. The wave-like aspect of our body is spread out throughout the universe. So it is just an idea we have that our body is located in space and has frontiers to its being. This is where science comes in and helps us confirm something we experience quite naturally in what is one of the most basic mystical experiences. The general assumption that everyone has is that particles, or persons, or bodies, are distributed at different points in space. But this is just one dimension of reality—what David Bohm calls the explicate order. In the implicate order, all particles exist as waves, interfusing with one another throughout space. In that sense, we can say that at one end of the scale we experience ourselves as separate bodies and separate individuals, and we communicate with other individuals who seem to be other than ourselves. But there is a dimension of our being in which we are all one and in which we communicate without thinking in terms of the other person being other than ourselves. There is no other, and there is no time and space.

Our thinking also fluctuates between these two extremes. For example, we can think of ourselves as being here, "me," consciousness—"I'm perceiving that tree which is over there" or "that person who is other than me and whose ideas are different from mine." But some of your thinking, mainly the intuitive thinking, is a kind of overall understanding that encloses many different thoughts—a global realization that is not made up of granulated thoughts, but in which all the thoughts seem to blend into one realization. There is thinking that is purely factual, but there is also a state of reverie, in which we ponder upon the meaningfulness of the situation. All the different thoughts are blended into an overall picture, which we can call the implicit form of thought we experience in meditation, when we have overcome the notion of time and space and all that remains is meaningfulness. You will notice that when this happens, you have lost the sense of yourself as an individual. In fact, as Buddha says, you reach a point where the word "me" doesn't make sense any longer. Those are the great moments. This is a wonderful experience that is completed when instead of just extending consciousness into the vastness, you actually penetrate into the consciousness of all beings. You contact beings through your consciousness, because it's all part of one consciousness, which is the divine consciousness. This is the cosmic dimension.

The other dimension is what is called the transcendental dimension. This is the second stage: getting into the thinking that has *become* the flower or the tree—the thinking of the divine order behind the universe. You see the whole physical universe as the crystallization of thought—the thought of the total being—and behind that the emotion of the total being, and behind that the consciousness of the total being. You can imagine the cosmic dimension as horizontal and the transcendental dimension as vertical. The transcendental dimension means entering into different levels of reality.

This, curiously enough, is what scientists are actually doing. For example, the shells of the atoms, which are the orbitals of the atoms, are described as electrons circling the nuclei of the atoms. These are placed according to harmonic, or mathematical, rules. Even if there is no electron in some of these shells, if an electron gets in the excited state, it will jump its orbit and get into a higher one—but the order in which it goes has been predetermined. This is an indication that mind is primary, rather than prior to matter; and it has primacy because the whole noetic reality—the order behind the universe—determines the pattern of things in the universe. The curious thing is that you can get into the consciousness of that order; and when you do, you discover a kind of harmony. What you experience is very similar to what Johann Sebastian Bach describes in his music, because he gets into the flow of the order behind the universe and it comes through in his music. It's a question of getting into a state of resonance with the order, so you start with beings like flowers and animals and so on, but eventually you can go beyond that and get into the order behind the universe. Then you see the difference between the thinking of a tree and the thinking that has become the tree.

If you walk in the forest, what do you see of the trees? You see only the bark of the tree; you have to get into the consciousness of the tree to experience the reality of that tree. The bark is just a very small part of the tree, and that's all you see. Behind that there is the consciousness that has become the tree. When you get into the consciousness that has become the tree, you are carried beyond your own understanding and you realize that beyond the understanding of the mind there is a sense of relationship, or *ratio*, which is the Latin root for rational thinking—although it has been totally deformed from its original etymology, which does not mean the same thing as logic. It has to do with a sense of proportion, like arithmetic progression, geometric progression, and harmonic progression. When you get into the order behind the universe, you discover very beautiful proportions and relationships—the pattern behind things, which is just the basis—and then it gets very complicated and elaborate. The inventiveness of it is beyond description.

You could compare it with a model of perpetual music that

repeats itself all the time, a little bit like the "Bolero" of Ravel, for example, although there is very little variety there compared with the extremely elaborate toccatas and fugues of Bach, in which there are three and sometimes four different themes that intermesh and coalesce and conjugate and form something new. So if you get behind the order of the universe, it's so exciting there is hardly any way of describing it.

But there is still something more, and that is the emotion behind the universe. When you get into that, you suddenly find a cosmic emotion underlying what you are experiencing through the senses. Eventually, you realize that your own emotions are really terribly unimportant. I've often wondered whether Mother Teresa has any personal problems—of course, everyone has—but I think they're just not very important for her; and I think there is a way of rising beyond one's personal tempests in a teacup and getting into the emotion of the cosmos. When you do that, your whole being is transformed.

Perhaps the most urgent need in a human being is for transformation—and in a practical and tangible way, which is to say in the personality. How do you bring about transformation in the personality? You can't bring it about by working on yourself and saying, "I don't have enough strength—I've got to work with power to become a little bit more powerful." It doesn't work that way. But once you've gotten into the emotion behind the universe, it transforms you altogether. You become sensitive to the sufferings and joys of people, and you can feel the dishonesty of people if they are dishonest or if they are trying to manipulate you. What is more, you see very clearly what you let yourself in for in life. Most of us don't realize just how we've gotten ourselves entangled in all kinds of situations. We have alienated our freedom, which is the most valuable thing in the world. And, of course, it's very difficult to extricate yourself once you've involved yourself.

So the transcendental dimension gives a kind of perspective from which you can look at your life with great objectivity.

This leads us to the question, "What exactly is transcendence?" One of the most fundamental beliefs we have when we use the word "God" is in a being whose body is the totality of the universe. We come to that realization when we look at our own bodies and realize that our bodies are made of the fabric of the planet and that we are participating in the nature of the planet in our bodies. The ancients used to say that the body is just something that is being borrowed, but it is also true that we are our bodies; it is just difficult for the mind to accept the possibility of being two different things at the same time. When I was studying logic at the university, I learned the syllogism, "Man is mortal; Socrates is a man; therefore, Socrates is mortal." That's logic; and according to logic, he couldn't be mortal and immortal at the same time. He must be either mortal or immortal. The Catholic Church did discount this logic by saying that Christ was both divine and human, but then they said it's a mystery. Today, scientists have come to the conclusion that it is the old-fashioned logic that stands in the way of our understanding phenomena—such as matter being both particle and wave at the same time.

In any case, the basic assumption most people have when they use the word "God" is that God is a being whose body is the physical universe, and the reality of whose being exists at all other levels—the level of a mental being, an emotional being, and so forth. This view is what is called immanence. Many theologians cannot accept that view for the simple reason that the universe is fraught with imperfection. How can you call that God? If all that you see is God, it becomes a problem, so that you might try to maintain transcendence and say, "No, this is just creation, and God is beyond creation." But you could make a comparison with the body and say that while the fingernails and hair are part of the body, they don't seem to be quite as intelligent as the cells in the brain, for example; there are differences in degree. You could consider the physical universe as ramification of the being of God, who is a very special core within this totality; and that is how you can maintain the concept of transcendence—although this is, of course, in the mind.

I do not know what kind of chemistry or concourse of circumstances makes it possible for a human being to have an experience of God, and I have been very wary of it because I've often wondered whether we didn't anthropomorphize or create God in our own image and ascribe to Him things we are conversant with. The experience of God is something you reach when you get into the consciousness of the order behind the universe and the emotion behind that order. You suddenly see God very clearly not as a principle but as a being. Of course, I am speaking from my own experience, and one might say, "Well, your experience was warped by your background or whatever." I know I'm on thin ice here: it is just something one has to realize for oneself when one comes to that point.

It is the sense of sacredness that gives you your conviction. This is a word we have forgotten in our time: we have lost the sense of the sacred. There are stories from the past of beings who are really sacred—for example, Father Seraphim, who was an Orthodox monk who lived in the eighteenth century and who left the official church and lived as a hermit in the forest. He used to shun people and would hide behind the trees when people came to find him—except that he would always come out if there were children, because he loved children. One day a man managed to find him, and said to him, "In the church they talk about the Holy Spirit, but what does it mean?" Father Seraphim dropped his woodcutter's hatchet, took the man by the shoulders, and shook him and shook him; and the man said there was so much light in the eyes of Father Seraphim that all of a sudden he felt a kind of jolt in his soul and he realized the Holy Spirit. This is a wonderful story, because we have ideas about spirituality, but spirituality is something that has to be experienced. And the only way to experience it is through a human being.

There are people who have become pure spirit. On an Indian pilgrimage, a group of us met the greatest rishi in India. He never visits anybody and is generally lost in samadhi, so even if you do go to see him you never have any contact with him. But he came to see us, and he just filled the whole room with his being, and we were moved to the depths of our being. You can't imagine what happens to a human being who has become so totally overwhelmed by the consciousness of God. He was in his late eighties; his body was a wreck; he only eats fruit. He couldn't walk, but he could dance. He goes into samadhi—a state of ecstasy—for three or four days. When he comes back, he asks if there is any food. They bring him an apple and put it in his hand, and after a few minutes he drops the apple and goes off into samadhi for another three or four days. Because of this way of life, he has become a channel for an extraordinary sacredness.

We try to encourage people in their spiritual ideals because one of the most precarious things in human beings is the hope that what they believe to be ideal is not just their imagination. This is why many people are scuttling themselves—they are convinced that what they believe in isn't true. That is the despair of the human being, and that is why spirituality is so important. But if we give people a kind of predigested, intellectual, unreal spirituality, it does more harm than good. One has to really live it. What is important is to see what it does to a human being. This is beyond belief: beyond belief there is real experience.

So the message I have for you is that you can have

experience. You must remember that experience is always interpreted, however; according to your experience, the sun moves around the earth, so that experience has to be re-interpreted for us to realize that it's the other way around: the earth moves around the sun. Just experience is not good enough. It has to be digested. What is much more serious is that experience is sometimes impeded by your mental background. Theses stand in the way of experience, so that as long as people continue to think the way they do, they may never have the experience. There are certain things we have to undo in our way of thinking before we can meditate.

First, we have to understand that the way things look depends upon our vantage point. Then we have to realize that our understanding is limited by logic—by the assumption that a thing cannot be both this and that at the same time. The old-fashioned method of attaining the experience of transcendence, which is used in India, is to watch your body and see that it is made of the fabric of the earth. Then you say, "How could I be bones and flesh and blood and heart? I can't be that; it's just come about this way—it's the way nature has worked things out. Why do I feel that that's me?" And you get detached from your identification with your body.

Then you watch your mind and think to yourself, "Well, that's the way the mind is made—why do I think it's my thoughts? Nature made the bodies of people similar, and in the same way nature made the thoughts of people very similar, so why do I think they're my thoughts?" You might then say, "Surely I've got a different opinion than other people—I have some kind of original thoughts." But you have an impact on your body: you can make that lump of flesh walk, and isn't that extraordinary? You have a very special relationship with that lump of flesh—you can't make other lumps of flesh walk. But that doesn't mean that you *are* that lump of flesh. In the same way, you have a special connection with your thinking.

I use the word "thinking" rather than "mind," because "mind" is a static word and "thinking" is a dynamic word. But you are not your mind, and the truth is that you can make your mind function, too.

Then you come to your personality and the inheritance from your ancestors—not just your parents; in fact, the whole universe has contributed toward the formation of this personality. That's the way nature did it. Can you say, "This is me"? According to the Hindus, you would have to say, "No, I'm not my personality. I'm not anything that is a formation." And I suppose that the reason for this is that somehow there is a sense that anything that has been formed will one day be destroyed, and when I say "I," somehow fundamentally I assume that I mean something permanent—at least in the Hindu philosophy. There is a sense of eternity in the human being, and so you can look upon everything that is transient as being not yourself, and try to cleave to that which is eternal. That is basically the Hindu and Buddhist approach.

In Christianity, we think differently, because the prospect of resurrection is so important. The Christian will reply to the Hindu, "No, things are not transient, because eventually that which has been formed is going to be eternalized—it's going to be transmuted and eternalized, and that is the meaning of resurrection." You might call this dogma; what, after all, is meant by it? Does it mean that the body is going to rise out of the tomb, as some people used to think? No; if you go deeply into it, you will realize what it really means. The best comparison is that if you have thousands of flowers, they will fade away, but if you are able to draw the perfume out of those flowers, the perfume will live forever. That is the meaning of resurrection.

Nothing is lost in the universe. That is a truism in science, and it is true in general. Whatever has been gained by your body—such as your face—even if it fades away as you get older, it can never be lost. It must be transmuted, of course. And if that is so, then that which the Hindus said was transient is not that transient. It's valid and it's worthwhile. It's going to survive, and therefore we cannot look upon our body and say that it is just the body. In fact, if you start getting into the consciousness of the body—the life of the cells, the intelligence of the cells, or even of the molecules or the electrons and the photons—you realize what a miracle the body is. It's a wonderful thing. And what is more, something has been gained by the fact that the mind has been able to infuse right into matter in the living body.

This is why we have a new approach now. We have to accept that we are both transient and eternal at the same time. And you can discover your eternity. It is really very easy to say, "My body is not me, and my mind is not me, and my personality is not me." And, of course, you also come to the critical point when you look upon your consciousness and realize that it too is just a formation—just an eddy in the ocean of consciousness. If you can identify yourself with the total consciousness—not a vantage point but overall consciousness—and then look upon your consciousness and see how things look from the vantage point of this limited consciousness, then you can realize that it has its relative value while you still see beyond it. This is a wonderful experience, and it's easy to experience transcendence if you use these methods.

But in reality, we are also our bodies and our minds and our personalities, and if you are able to get into the divine consciousness without being limited by the personal vantage point, that is the answer. The new methods of meditation do not lead to an escape from reality, like lifting one's consciousness into a sort of abstract state, but involve getting right down into the divine consciousness and seeing what's happening in the universe, in oneself. Hazrat Inayat Khan

said that God enjoys discovering Himself in the perfect human
being. So you could say that our purpose is to become as much
as possible the expression of the divine inheritance, so that we
are able to manifest it to view.

When we spoke about the personality, we said that it had
been constructed in the course of time. It's the inheritance
from your parents and your ancestors, and there are many
other factors—angelic ancestors, previous incarnations
possibly—but most important is your divine inheritance.
When Christ said, "Be ye perfect as your Father in heaven is
perfect," he meant that you have the divine inheritance in
you, and that you have to be conscious of your inheritance.
We inherit divine perfection. This is where our understanding
gets in the way: we assume that we are a fraction of the
totality, and it is very difficult to understand that we are both
a fraction of the totality *and* the totality.

How do we make that perfect inheritance a reality? The
answer is that to become what you are, you have to see yourself
in another yourself who is more able to manifest what you are
than yourself. You have it in you, but you have to see it in
order to become it, and that is why we are continually looking
for ourselves in another ourself—in other people. When you
see qualities that are present in you in another person, it gives
you the courage to be like that. You see that it's actually
possible. Otherwise you doubt that you could be like that,
because it seems like too much of an ideal; it doesn't seem
real. That's the reason for the popularity of the charismatic
guru these days—although in the Sufi tradition, as Jalal
ad-din Rumi said, the pir-o-murshid destroys the idol that
people make of him.

Plotinus said, "That which one fails to experience in
contemplation, one tries to experience outside"—but it's all
inside. God is present in the secret chamber of the heart. But
you have to see Him in the sunrise and in the power of the

elephant, in the fluttering of the birds and in a wonderful person, in music and in all those things that express something that is already in you and reveals yourself to yourself. That is the principle of meditation.

CHAPTER 8

# The Fulfillment
# of God's Purpose

I feel we are all involved in the dichotomy between the way of the sannyasin and the way of fulfillment in life. It's almost inbred. When I come back from a retreat, I feel I've gotten into a place where I become very sensitive to the pollution and to the egotism and brashness and vulgarity of people, so that I feel I'm only really happy and in harmony with the environment when I'm sitting in the woods or on a mountain top. From that vantage point, there's a feeling that we've so completely denatured the environment that for a very sensitive person it's almost unlivable.

On the other hand, many of us not only have a sense of responsibility, but also enjoy life and those things that are fulfilled in activity—the great achievements of mankind. I myself am glad we have a car, and I know that means that people have to work very hard in the factories to make it possible. And I'm glad we have a tape recorder so that we can listen to music without having to go to a concert each time, which would be difficult. And I'm glad to have a nice shampoo in the morning. I'm glad to see all that has resulted from the skills of men and their incentives: the great cities and what they represent—the amount of hard work and dedication and discipline and overcoming that it all represents. And what is more, it's the easy way to go and sit in the woods. We are called upon to bring spirituality into everyday life. We can consider a retreat to be a little holiday from this very hard task; being able to sit in the woods is a little holiday. But most of our time is not spent sitting in the woods, so the question is, how are we preparing ourselves while sitting in the woods for what we're doing in everyday life?

This dichotomy goes much farther, of course. It was threaded throughout one of my retreats, when I felt a great need to experience samadhi and the Buddhist meditations—to reach beyond life into the source of life. You can never be the same once you've seen beyond the curtain, and there's no doubt that we should begin by doing this. Then, of course, there are Sufi practices that help you to see the meaningfulness of all that is attained and achieved in the universe. If you do these different practices and see how they work upon you, then the whole thing becomes clear. It's important to be able to feel exactly your attunement—your spiritual attunement—and the way you can just switch this attunement; you should be able even to introduce the way of renunciation while being active. You're not necessarily in one state or the other. Ultimately you should be able to combine the two. But before we can combine the two, we must no doubt experience each one very deeply.

For example, we've polluted the planet. Even the minds of people have become polluted. This is partly what has caused the wish to go back to nature and to be a sannyasin; if you're living in an artificial house that is insulated by artificial material, you're cutting out a lot of forms of energy in nature, such as the cosmic energy that is cut out by your roof. But you can find that you have access to another form of energy. You can sit in a skyscraper in New York City and have access to a very high form of energy that does not depend upon the earth—a different level of energy. Civilization has its disadvantages, but it does not prevent anyone from living a spiritual life.

In fact, nowadays it's a much greater achievement to be able to bring spirituality into everyday life. That is the message of our time, and that was the work of Hazrat Inayat Khan. If you go through his teachings, you'll see that occasionally he gives expression to a longing for solitude. This strikes a chord in us, because we all feel like that. At the end of his life, he was walking along the Jumna in Delhi and saw a sannyasin sitting in a hut. Murshid greeted him, and there was a marvelous empathy between those two. And Murshid told the *mureed* ("disciple") who was with him that he could have chosen this way, but he chose instead to go to the West. For an easterner, this is especially difficult, because the attitude of the eastern disciple is very different. I often see people coming up to me with their hands in their pockets or cigarettes in their mouths, or lying down with their feet turned towards me. In the East they would never do such a thing; you don't find people coming up to you and saying, "Do you know about such and such?" So Murshid must have been very shocked at times. He went through some really hard things, including even racial prejudice.

So we know that when we have once experienced the ecstasy of solitude and samadhi, it's something so meaningful that it can make it really difficult to deal with everyday things. On the other hand, if you are able to overcome your leaning towards solitude and see the whole purpose behind what is achieved, then of course everything falls into place. This is why Murshid places so much emphasis on being able to experience the divine consciousness in manifestation. There is a sense of the divine purpose being fulfilled in the consciousness of the divine Being—the ecstasy of the divine Being manifesting.

Hazrat Inayat Khan speaks of two awakenings. He says there is awakening in the sleep in the night of time and awakening at the surface in the world, the manifested realm. We tend to go a little bit overboard in turning away from the artificial life we're leading. There are a lot of things in our lives that are not in harmony with nature. The big issue, however, is not to let ourselves be trapped in the immediate environment—to be able to keep the expanse of consciousness wide; and not to let ourselves be trapped in our sense of limitation, but keep our consciousness high. The key to this can be found in the words of Hazrat Inayat Khan, when he says that whether the dervish is living in a hut or a palace, he's always a king. It's not the place where you live that is going to make the ultimate difference. It's your consciousness that does it. Whether you're chopping wood, conducting a choir, washing up, typing, or working in a factory, you can still be a king or a queen. It's a matter of your awareness of your divine inheritance.

Our problem is that we are all caught up in identifying ourselves with our limitation, so naturally we have a sense of inadequacy. When Murshid says you're a king, it sounds like an ego trip until you are really aware of that dimension of your being that is eternal—the eternity of your being. Then all of a sudden there's a change in your awareness. It doesn't mean that you have pride in your ego; rather, there is a sense of the dignity of your inheritance, your divine inheritance. It's very important when we're facing problems—especially when we're facing ourselves and our own sense of inadequacy—to be able to have access to this transcendental awareness, which helps keep us from getting caught in the ultimate illusion, which is limitation.

The Sufi meditations lead to just this realization, which is where they differ from the samadhi of the Hindus or the *sattipatana* of the Buddhists. Hazrat Inayat Khan suggests several Sufi practices that give you a sense of your kingly inheritance. For instance, you discover in yourself the very power that moves the universe—the same power that moves the planets and galaxies, the molecules and atoms, and the sap in the trees; the power that divides the cells of the living organism and causes the embryo to grow, and that brings a person to the point of becoming a hero or a martyr or to stand up for his ideals. It is not a personal power, but a kind of power beyond the frame of the ego. It is the power that gives mastery: for example, you can use it to overcome impulses or give them direction. It is the power through which you can harness impulses, get yourself together and hold the reins of your own being. It makes it possible for you to control situations so they don't get out of hand; ultimately it makes it possible for you to assume responsibility. It's something that we've inherited from our eternal being.

Another thing Murshid talks about is a certain type of attunement, which we call ecstasy. We all know ecstasy as it is triggered off by circumstances. A football match, climbing the mountains, hang gliding, listening to music, being in love, forgiving someone who has offended you—all these things give ecstasy. Giving up something that you want very much, or risking your life to save someone, gives ecstasy; being detached gives ecstasy. These are the kinds of ecstasy that are provoked by circumstances or that you can bring about by intervening in circumstances. But Murshid is speaking about a totally different dimension of ecstasy that is not something that rises out of that part of your being that is temporary or transient, but that comes from the very root of your being— that dimension that is eternal. That is when you are able to feel in yourself the depth, the condition of the universe. It's not like what you experience through your senses or through your mind. You discover it right in your very bones—in the very depths of your being. Ecstasy is the inheritance of the soul. It doesn't depend on circumstances. It's the ultimate form of energy—an overwhelming psychic energy that gives you a tremendous power to do things. There's nothing that acts more strongly upon people—and even upon animals and plants. Just imagine being able to touch upon the condition of the whole universe. That's what Hazrat Inayat Khan was talking about when he described a rishi sitting in the mountain fastness and said that the whole of nature was caught in his ecstasy. In that case, you're not dependent on the environment: you can sit in a hotel room or a bar, in a train—anywhere, even in prison, as did Baha'ullah—and you're not enclosed in the immediate environment. In fact, the only way to have access to this cosmic energy is not to allow yourself to be enclosed in the immediate environment. That's the great secret. The environment can lock you into a very narrow area. If you keep your consciousness vast, you feel the condition of the whole universe, not just the environment.

You experience the environment through your senses and your mind, but you experience the whole universe by that deeper root of your being that I call the eternal aspect. The secret of this is to imagine the consciousness of the One Being whose body is the universe. What must be the ecstasy of the consciousness whose body is the galaxies and the nebulae, the stardust and the comets and the quasars and the black holes—all the atoms and molecules? Imagine the ecstasy of that consciousness, and remember that the roots of your consciousness plunge into that consciousness. You're just like a ramification of that consciousness, and you can move right back into it. That is the consciousness of the dervish. Many rishis may experience it, but it is not typical of the consciousness of the rishi. It is the consciousness of the dervish.

You can draw a lot of energy from the environment if you're sitting in a natural environment, or even walking or lying in a natural environment. But we have the capacity to draw energy from the vastness beyond the environment, and you can sit in a room and have access to this energy. It's a matter of the setting of the consciousness, and this is what is meant by *prana*. The energy at the bottom of the spine is certainly enhanced if you're sitting on the earth, because it's an earth energy; it may be the magnetism of the geomagnetic field. In any case, it's a very material and tangible form of energy that can be transmuted as it is drawn up along the spinal cord. It's a very wonderful thing to be able to do that. But there is also the energy that you get through the solar plexus, and that is not dependent on the environment. You can be anywhere and draw that energy towards you. It's a matter of expanding consciousness into the vastness of space.

We don't even know what space is really; some scientists think that space is a void, and others are now beginning to feel that it is all filled with neutrinos and what is between the neutrinos. What we're speaking about is the space of matter, from which matter is derived; and, of course, beyond this space is the space of space. So the kind of energy we're talking about is probably not just the energy such as is measured by scientists as it gets transformed into matter and as matter gets re-transformed into energy. It's something more basic than that, although it is not quite what is meant by spirit. I would say that it is the cosmic dimension of energy, whereas spirit is the transcendental. If you expand your consciousness—not just thinking of the vastness of space as it looks from your vantage point, but reaching out into all points of space at the same time, scattering your consicousness throughout the vastness of space so that consciousness is decentered—that is where you have access to *prana*. As you inhale, you draw energy into the heart center and the solar plexus, and the amount of energy that you are able to draw in is a function of the setting of consciousness. If the consciousness is set at a very wide scale and is decentered, you have access to much more energy.

The next form of energy that we have access to is what we call "the spirit," and the crown *chakra*, the subtle energy center at the top of the head, is the most appropriate instrument through which it can be experienced. Sometimes we call it "celestial energy" or "transcendental energy." Transcendental means beyond the beyond—the Sanskrit *parat param*. So the meaning of transcendence is that it is always beyond anything that we could ever fathom, and it comes when we can clearly see the physical world as being a materialization or concretization or existentiation or crystallization of pure spirit. In order to reach this energy, you have to abandon your concept of yourself as being bodily; you have to be bodiless, ethereal, spaceless, timeless. You have to let go of the gravity pull that brings you down into ego-consciousness and the solidity of the body. Then your whole attunement is different: you become pure spirit. You can feel that you're attuned to a different type of energy. The earth power seems to move up the spinal cord, whereas this energy moves down. It's an incredible energy; it's difficult to see how it works its way down into manifestation. It's not like the power that makes you face problems: it's the power behind power, the catalyst. It may trigger off a power that's more tangible. It makes you sensitive and may alienate you a little from people; you may find it difficult to deal with the world. But it does give you the power to heal, and it's only when you're attuned to the Holy Spirit that you can approach people on their deathbeds and help them rather than disturb them by your presence. It's the only attunement that can enable you to approach the holy of holies, the burning bush.

The attunement of this energy—there's an emotional attunement corresponding to each kind of energy—is sobriety rather than ecstasy. It's not the euphoria or enthusiasm that is experienced in fulfillment in life, but rather the kind of emotion that is experienced when you have overcome all things and freed yourself from all desires. Now, the basic problem is how to introduce this very fine form of energy into life. It's not the kind of energy that can protect you against brutality or that you can apply in the form in which it is to achieving things, but it could trigger off forms of energy that lead toward achievement, fulfillment, building, creativity, and motivation. It's the secret power in the background. If you don't have it, you might tend to get carried away by your own enthusiasm.

This is where we find the ability to introduce the way of the sannyasin into the middle of life. As Murshid says, achievement gives power, but renunciation gives still more power. There's a time for achievement and a time for renunciation. What we are trying to do is to introduce renunciation in the middle of achievement. If you renounce the fruit of action, you can be very active without being bogged down in the satisfaction of what you get out of it. You can have the emotion of sobriety, which is beyond all emotion, and at the same time the joy of fulfillment and accomplishment. It's a very nice balance.

Finally, we can learn to get into the realization of the total being. Our understanding accrues to us through our experience of communication with the physical world and the mind world. But behind this understanding that accrues from outside—the transient aspect of our being—there is a realization that belongs to the permanent root of our being and that does not accrue through experience, but is inborn. Of course, there must be some form of communication between these two forms of knowledge. Our inborn realization is continually up against our understanding, and if something were not gained by existence, then our understanding would not in any way contribute towards our realization. Our deeper realization must benefit by our understanding. But as Murshid says, if you start getting into the consciousness of the divine Being in action, then you begin to see the cause behind the cause behind the cause and the purpose beyond the purpose beyond the purpose. The understanding sees a cause; inference sees a cause. The way of realization is to see the cause behind the cause and the motive beyond the motive: you don't stop at your rational inferences. Consciousness is always working at a higher dimension, never caught in the limitation of argument or rational inference. You have to call upon the whole other dimension of your being. In fact, this is what is meant by divine consciousness.

The ramification of your consciousness is a projection out of the total consciousness. So the attainment of realization is a matter of drawing back into the source of your understanding. Hazrat Inayat Khan puts it very well when he says that we're continually drawn to the surface of life where things are happening, but the causes are in the depth. This is why we say that a sage is deep: his energy always comes from a deep place. It is a matter of not being judgmental or opinionated. You overcome what Buddha calls "the bramble of opinion"; in fact, the word "orthodoxy" is from the Greek for "true opinion." Realization is beyond opinion, beyond the judgment of the mind. It's the point at which everything suddenly makes sense.

You really have to stretch your understanding into its infinite dimensions. In fact, the eternal dimension is like the substratum out of which the temporary is projected: you could say that the realization is the foundation out of which the understanding emerges. So you don't discard your understanding; you reach into its foundations. Our minds think "I" and think of the divine consciousness as being something else. If you realize that the divine consciousness is the very depth from which you emerge, then it becomes easier. You háve always to get over the sense of the otherness of God, which is a very dangerous concept.

Finally, you can clearly see your personality as emerging out of the divine nature. Your personality also has its roots in the divine nature; it's not something that is arrested in its growth; it's not a separate entity. It's linked, it has its roots in its foundation, and it's growing. What is more, while you can identify with your personality, you can also draw back into the roots of your personality and find as you get farther back into the roots that the qualities seem to be more and more perfect. For example, you may have a certain amount of compassion, a certain amount of patience, a certain amount of truthfulness, a certain amount of purity, a certain amount of joy, and so forth, but these may all be limited: as we know, some people make it very difficult for us to love them. Yet somehow, when you draw back into the roots, you discover unlimited potential in your qualities—and there's no frontier between the roots of your personality and your personality. It's all one thing. Your personality grows out of that foundation that is common to all beings. This is the secret: not enclosing yourself in your concept of your limitation and then thinking that God is perfect, but seeing that it is all one totality that gets limited at one end but is linked with the perfection, so that as you draw back you become aware of the perfection of all those qualities that you think are imperfect in your being.

When we do the practice of *dhikr* it's the total being who emerges in each being—the totality of the total being emerges in each fraction of the total being. When you see that, you see what Hazrat Inayat Khan means about becoming aware of the divine inheritance—it becomes very real. These are typical Sufi practices without mantrams, *wazifas*, or the *dhikr*, with the aid of Murshid's thoughts, that can bring about a total change of outlook and a total conversion of our being, cutting into the very foundations of our existence and correcting some of the most widely accepted assumptions that are standing in the way of our spiritual unfoldment—or even of our unfoldment generally. It's not samadhi and it's not *sattipatana;* it's the kind of meditation that is emerging now in the light of Sufism as it has come through in the West through Hazrat Inayat Khan.

CHAPTER 9

# "Why Do You Seek for God Up There? He Is Here!"

The dervish is in the world and yet not of the world. He sees all things happening, and yet he knows that they are not the way they look. He sees the invisible threads behind the actions of people, pulling them in different directions like puppets. For him, everything is paradoxical: there is a gain in every loss and a loss in every gain. He sees people drawn up into the high heavens and down into the dark depths of the nether worlds; and he sees in all manifestations the one living God who works in mysterious ways.

He sees how people are caught up in the illusion of their lives and fail to see the hand of God working beyond all things. He drinks the poison of love as a nectar that gives him ecstasy, and he is so in love with God that he sees in everyone the divine Beloved. He is so intoxicated by love that he is incurable. Except for the Beloved, what is there to see?

He goes places, and yet he knows that he is not going anywhere: it is just the body that is going somewhere; he realizes that he does not need feet to walk.

His soul is flying into the heavens and yet conscious of the reflection of the heavens on the earth; he is never completely unaware of that magic whereby God becomes a reality on earth. His very being is nostalgia, and yet he realizes that what he thinks is his nostalgia is the very nostalgia of God, in which God longs to see Himself in another himself. He realizes that he is the one in whom God sees Himself, and that therefore he has to exist, although he would like to die. He has to exist to be a mirror in which God can see Himself.

He knows that so long as there is any fragment of his own ego consciousness, God's vision of Himself through him is limited by his own limitation; he realizes that he can only be a perfect instrument of God's vision if he is just suspended between life and death. He is the living dead. Wherever he goes, he brings life, and yet within himself he is dead to himself—he is *fana,* annihilated. If people call his name, he feels like saying "Whom do you mean?" When people call on Allah, he says, "Yes?" Yet there is no presumption in his answer, because he could only be aware of the divine presence by not being aware of himself as a being; he sees himself as a transient existence that is continually recurring, and so much in the hands of God that it has no existence in itself. As a result, he sees without eyes, into the hearts of men—he sees their truth and their dishonesty, and he sees their intentions, their aspirations, and their fears. He sees the whole drama of life in each droplet of the ocean of creation, and he sees it all working towards a great fulfillment.

The dervish experiences the pleasure and displeasure of God in the intentions of man; he sees God dethroned by the blasphemy of men and he sees God's love betrayed by those who profess religion. He sees God handing himself into the hands of traitors in an act of love. And yet he realizes the overwhelming power of God that is stronger than the greatest power that any creature could ever wield, and he sees how the hand of God strikes in destiny, sometimes with such force that one is shattered by His presence. In other words, the dervish is faced with the consternation of intelligence. He pits his understanding against life until he abandons all sense of understanding, and then the divine understanding comes through. He would like to describe it and communicate it, but how can he do this? Who is going to understand the un-understandable? Who is going to understand the madness of one who has lost his mind in the realization of God? The mind is unable to function at these levels; it can only emit irrational exclamations and professions of love and ecstasy that make no sense to the ordinary mind.

The voice of the dervish is the voice of silence. He realizes that the more people speak, the less they are able to say, and his silence is more eloquent than the words of the greatest orator. He communicates the vibrations of the music of the spheres, and all beings are harmonized by that universal harmony: people are disarmed by his presence. They can come to him with their schemes, like the scorpions and snakes under the throne that Murshid mentions, but when they come into his presence they lose their self-confidence, because his power is the power of truth, which is the greatest power there is. The truth does not have to utter a word; it is just there. It speaks of itself; it is the open book of the scripture of life. It is like the light of the sun.

The dervish sees how people are afraid to look into the light, exactly as they are afraid of facing the truth. That is why some people keep a distance from him: they are afraid of his power —in fact, they are afraid of the power of God—to such an extent that he shields people from the power of his being and appears like an innocent child who plays with the children of the earth like a child and enjoys their games. He understands their guile and their misdemeanors; it's all part of growing up and it's all being planned. He sees the role of the devil, who is accomplishing his task of testing. How could we be tested if it were not for the devil in each one of us? The dervish sees the great battle being enacted in the heart of each man and woman. The devil is the sacrificed one, and he enjoys his role because it gives satisfaction to the ego—until he hangs himself by that same rope, because of the latitude he was given to intervene in the order of the universe by creating disorder.

So the dervish is the great observer of life. He does not withdraw from the living scene of life; he commits himself in the extreme. He lets his feet be chained with heavy chains and he lets his hands be chained or even allows himself to be laid upon a cross—and yet he is freer than any other human being, because no chains can ever limit the breadth of his consciousness and no suffering can ever take away one iota of his joy. He will say, as dervishes have said in the past, "They thought they crucified Jesus—what a hoax! They only grabbed his body—and even that escaped them. They think they can defy the divine will, they think they can intervene in the divine plan, they think they can defile the divine sanctity—what a hoax!"

Things are different from the way they look. People build up illusions out of packs of cards, fragile constructions of their minds and their wills that break down ignominiously when faced with the hand of God. The dervish becomes a king by his consciousness of the majesty of God. He is a king in beggar's robes, a king in patched robes, because he realizes the complete and utter nonexistence of himself and his own power. He has utter humility; and only those who have this humility dare wield the divine power. Only those who cease to have arrogance of mind dare wield the divine understanding, and only those who have lost all sense of the ego may wield the divine love.

If you can live in a cave, and if you think it is a good idea to live in a cave and leave the world, then you follow the path of the rishi. But if you find that you have to live in the world, and if you think that God has a purpose in His creation, then you become a dervish. You don't let yourself be upset by circumstances, you don't let yourself be conditioned by conditions, you don't take things at their face value, you don't judge human beings, you don't use your own power, you don't affirm your ego, and you don't hate any being. You merely watch things from the high pinnacle of the divine consciousness. Can you do this as you meditate? Can you just see yourself as you meditate as a purely transient creation that is destined to make God a reality on earth? Don't think of yourself as an illusion; think of yourself as being so fragile that you are completely dependent upon God. Think of yourself as being a temporary projection of God that exists in order to enable Him to see Himself: you are the beloved through whom He becomes the Lover, you are the object of His adoration. Then He becomes the object of your adoration. To be more precise, you are the object of His love, and He becomes the object of your adoration. And you are created out of His love. There is nothing more creative than love: it creates a being out of nothingness. Love is always a gift of oneself, of one's whole being to another; and so God gives Himself *into* you. He does not give Himself *to* you, because you don't exist except through this act of love; His gift of Himself becomes you.

And so the dervish, instead of looking for God up there, sees God down here. He realizes that his nostalgia for God seems to be a reflection of God's nostalgia for the love and vision of Himself through the person. The dervish never thinks of himself as the one who has nostalgia. It is God who is the Seer, God who is the Lover, and God who has the nostalgia, the yearning, the longing that sets anything static into dynamic motion. If you follow the path of the dervish, you are bewildered: you watch yourself with such amazement, because you see in yourself the manifestation of the very One you love—the very One whose love you experience in your love for Him. And you are amazed by the people you meet, because you see in them the expression of that very same love.

There are times when the dervish's soul is carried far beyond the world by an act of God whereby God isolates him in the solitude of His unity; just for the flash of a second God reveals to him His transcendence and obliterates His immanence. During that moment, the dervish carries all beings in his being as they are integrated and finally unified by the stem of the divine unity. When he returns from that state, then he begins to see unity in all diversity—just as, when he was in that state, he saw diversity in unity. He realizes that when you are looking at diversity, you cannot see the unity, and when you are looking at unity, you cannot see the diversity. But if you are suspended between the two, then you see the unity in diversity and the diversity in unity, and you see God resolving all the multiplicity in his unity and then again casting the bounty of his manifold forms into manifestation.

The dervish sees this happening in the lives of people—how at some times so much grace is given to them, and at others it is taken away. The person himself is perplexed and wonders why sometimes the sun shines upon him while at other times he seems to be the object of God's wrath or curse; the dervish sees this as the breath of God, inhaling and exhaling. If people would let themselves be drawn into the solitude of the divine unity when God draws them out of their unfoldment in the manifest, they would realize it as a higher initiation instead of regretting it and considering it to be an injustice of destiny. That is why the dervish accepts every gain as a gift of God and also every loss as a gift of God, like al-Hallaj, who said, "Even when I am deserted by you this isolation is a companion for me. Does not God try those whom He loves?"

This is meditation in action—but what action, and what a

meditation! There is no sense of isolation, no sense of having achieved anything, and no sense of superiority. There is a sense of complete dedication to the reality of God; there is a sense of total annihilation, and at the same time an upliftment and a power and insight beyond anything one could ever describe. This is the fundamental theme of the dervish: he walks without feet, flies without wings, sees without eyes, and speaks in silence. He is the instrument of the divine vision when he is no more there to see, and he is the instrument of the divine love when he is no more there to love. His life is suspended beyond life and death—he is the living death. Whatever affects him affects all beings, and whatever affects all beings affects him.

# CHAPTER 10

# "Walk Without Feet
# and Fly Without Wings"

The more deeply we experience life, the more deeply we are shaken by all that is happening to ourselves and to other people. We would so like to know why things happen the way they do. If you can enter into the despair in the hearts of people who are suddenly faced with a disaster that seems totally incomprehensible and unaccountable, and then find yourself faced with the sudden bounty of the divine grace, when sunshine seems to illuminate your life, you very naturally ask, "What is it all about?"

In some ways, we seem to be undergoing a process of death—not in the sense of an event that takes place at a certain moment of our lives, but as a process that seems to be happening all the time. We experience the death of our aspirations and our hopes, which are then replaced by other hopes, some of which are much farther off. There seems to be a continuous struggle for the survival of the eternal aspect of our being beyond the temporary one, which seems to have to dissolve. We are called upon to show readiness to let go of all those things that have to undergo dissolution so that we may survive in our real being, which is immortal.

We could look upon our whole sojourn on the planet as a great pilgrimage that is moving on an unknown path, toward horizons that seem to recede the farther we advance. The path is marked by thresholds, so that at a certain moment we feel that we've reached our destination—but then all of a sudden all of those values that we had built up in our fragile mental constructions tumble down like a house of cards, and we find ourselves going through a dark night, then crossing the threshold and finding ourselves with a completely new outlook and with fresh energy. Everything seems to be fine until we pass another threshold and find ourselves again at a point where we realize that we are reaching out for things that are beyond the grasp of our mind, and there is a kind of collapse of our mind before the enormity of what we are discovering—until we realize that all progress can only take place as a consequence of the shattering of all the stilted formations that have been built up.

The formula in alchemy is *solve et coagula*—things dissolve, and then there is a new coagulation, a new kind of stratification, that takes place; and this in turn has to break down so that further progress is possible. If we stayed the way we are, then of course we would never progress, so we just have to enjoy this process. Every new discovery shatters us, and that shattering is part of our re-creation.

Our ignorance is the best protection against what would happen if we faced reality without protection. Do you have the courage to face reality? We would all like to know reality—to sense or feel it—but we feel helpless when we are standing face to face with the force of destiny. If you were to look at the sun for more than a few seconds, your retina would be completely burned, but there are rishis in India who look at the sun from sunrise to sunset without blinking their eyelids for one minute. There is a great difference between us in our capacity to face reality. Al-Hallaj said that if only you could ever come across the divine understanding, your understanding would be totally shattered. Jalal ad-din Rumi said, "The secret of all truth is hidden . . . . If I spoke openly of it, the world would be overthrown." And Ibn al-'Arabi said, "One atom of the plane where He functions would shatter the world."

We are secure in our little constructions, our houses, our lives, our insurance policies, and so forth. Do we have the courage to go out into outer space, where our whole sense of ourselves is obliterated completely? And do we have the courage to be ourselves? Do we have the courage to be completely truthful? We think we are truthful, and then we compromise with the truth. It would make our lives very difficult to be completely truthful—and yet it is just that truth that makes a being. The strongest beings are beings of truth.

I was walking in the streets of Hardwar in India, where they were preparing for the great Kumbh Mela, which is a gathering of holy people that takes place every twelve years. Many, many people are going to India just looking for gurus, and most of them come back and say that they did not meet anyone particularly impressive. That is true; how could they? The great ones are hidden in the caves. You can't see them. But they all come down for the Kumbh Mela once every twelve years, and there they are. It's incredible. And as I was walking down the street, I saw a man walking there just like the king of kings. You simply wouldn't believe what that being was like. He had an enormous curved staff like the staff of Moses in one hand and a beggar's bowl in the other, and he was dressed in rags; and the power of his eyes was incredible. He was followed by an army of about fifty rishis—men who have lived in caves for thirty or forty years. I thought of the rest of us humans and our petty little lives—our tempests in our teacups and our struggles with our little daily affairs. We have no idea of the greatness of a human being when he is really tackling the great values of life. The conduct of most of our lives is really a terrible waste of human initiative and human power.

What are we fulfilling in our lives? Our lifetime is a unique opportunity, and what are we doing with it? Fortunately, there is something in us that feels stifled by our ordinary lives and is seeking something beyond. There is a nostalgia that is the greatest thing in us—our nostalgia for perfection, our intuition of wider dimensions of reality, and our resolve to reach them at all costs. That is where we are tested in our mental resolve—in our ability to stand for what we really believe in—and it is so much easier to compromise. This is not necessarily true only in the outer things. Often we think that just changing the circumstances of our lives will do it—but it doesn't do it. That's not where the problem lies.

Of course, you do have to make your life. You have to build your heaven, and then people have to adjust to the heaven you have built instead of your fitting yourself to their hell. It takes a lot of fortitude and a lot of power just to impose your heaven so that people have to take it or leave it. You build your own atmosphere. We have a sense of trying to reach a place, but Shems-i Tabriz says, "Walk without feet and fly without wings." We think we need feet to walk and that we can get somewhere by going somewhere. Buddha says, "There is a place that you cannot reach by going anywhere." We don't realize that we don't need to have wings to fly; it is our aspiration for the divine that lifts our consciousness upwards, but we don't use those wings. And we would like to see without eyes, if we only knew how much better we can see without eyes: we can see right into the hearts of people, which is something we cannot do with our eyes, because people wear a mask. And yet we are gifted with the ability to peer right into the hearts of people.

It is really the nostalgia for divine perfection that makes us look for it in people. You cannot see it if you don't assume that it is there: if you are not looking for it, there's a tendency to assume that it isn't there. If you're looking for a four-leaf clover, you're more likely to find one; if you are not looking, you might walk right over it and never see it.

What makes the dervish is what is called the "state of intoxication of the dervish"—the discovery of meaningfulness that is so shattering to the mind and the understanding and the heart that one is just overwhelmed by it. There are other people who just walk through it all and don't see it. We discover that the way things look to our understanding is absolutely preposterous. The brute, the unscrupulous and dishonest person, seems to succeed and get away with everything, and the person who is following his highest ideal and sacrificing himself for his ideal is victimized and insulted and despised. It is difficult to see that there is any justice or any pattern—any programming in the whole thing.

A scientist sees some kind of planning in everything. There are very few cases where the programming seems to be contradictory. But in the case of the events of our lives, we find it difficult to see the programming—because, obviously, we cannot be objective. But suppose we were able to look upon ourselves as an object instead of a subject. Suppose we could just watch our lives happening instead of being right down in them and caught up in the events, taking things at face value and missing the great show—the choreography of the heavens. If we could really see ourselves, we would see that there is something in us that is the pilgrim, or the visitor to the planet from outer space—and whatever that is, how personal is it? That is the meaning of *maya*—that I think I am a person until I begin to look at myself more clearly, and then I don't see where I begin and where I end. Teilhard de Chardin speaks of threads converging from all parts of space into a point. Is the human being that point, or is he the totality of all the threads? What does "I" mean in the whole thing? It is baffling to the mind. You get to a point where your whole viewpoint changes: you don't look upon things from the vantage point of the individual, because you doubt that there is such a thing. So you are prepared to abandon that vantage point. It is an extraordinary thing—like leaving yourself back home in your house and going out from what you thought you were into some other sphere that your personal consciousness cannot reach. That is what I mean by seeing without eyes. It is really experiencing without ego.

Those moments when we are uplifted are the moments when we have the strength to abandon our ego selves. This usually occurs when we are moved by a very strong emotion that is so meaningful that we are absolutely staggered. Meaning, when it strikes us very strongly, shatters us in our emotions. We cannot describe it, because we just make it intellectual. And this is what people are sensing more and more: those further reaches of emotion that are found when we have the courage to fare beyond the limits of the mind.

There is nothing more transforming that ecstasy. It is like the sunshine that brings all the seeds to fruition; it is the sunshine in the unfoldment of your being. First of all, of course, we unfold ourselves in our confrontation with reality; we discover ourselves in another person or in the sunrise or in the moon, in the thunder and lightning or the waterfall or the frigid northern scene. We discover different aspects of ourselves in those things that seem to be outside ourselves but are really not outside ourselves. As long as we think of ourselves as individual beings, we are continually gaining the courage to be ourselves by seeing ourselves in other beings who are more ourselves than we have the courage to affirm in our own existence. And it is, ultimately, a question of courage—of having confidence in your real being, which is ultimately, of course, the divine Being.

Belief in God can become very sterile, and many people are moving away from it because it is presented in the wrong way, as a dogmatic concept in which people are required to believe. But we are continually seeking to sense that unknown factor behind our lives, or underlying our lives—the "point omega." We sense that there is something else that is beyond all that is happening and that is continually projecting itself in our existences, and we want to relate to it. But how are we able to do so?

Farid ad-din Attar once said, "You are your own jailer." Do you think you are not free? You are free, but you do not know that you are free—and it is your not knowing that you are free that is your limitation and your imprisonment. Realize your freedom and you are free. In the same way, how can you be radiant if you do not realize that your are God? If you think of yourself as a human being, you have every reason not to be radiant. Probably there are people who have been terribly mean to you; everything goes wrong, and so on. So it is really going to be difficult to be radiant if you identify yourself with your person; but if you realize that what you thought was a person just doesn't exist, then you reach a new phase. You are able to look upon yourself as the eyes through which God sees. (This is the way the Sufi says it.) You cease to think that you are yourself the person who sees and become aware of a more encompassing intelligence that is functioning through you. You assume a perceptive attitude towards an active intelligence working through you, and this establishes a relationship with this unknown factor we call "God."

For instance, you might find yourself looking at children playing and it might suddenly occur to you, "That's not 'me' looking at these children—that's ridiculous. What is 'me'?" And then you discover the intelligence that is looking through your eyes, and you realize that that intelligence is *absolutely limitless*. There is no reason why you should just see the surface of the children's play. If you can see the whole cosmos, the dance of Shiva, in the play of the children, then they are enacting something cosmic and you are not limited to this scene: you let the light of the divine intelligence illuminate the whole scene from above. It is just like looking at a lake from the mountain top, where you can see the depth, instead of from the shores of the lake where you can only see the surface.

This is one of the states, or *maqams*, recognized by the Sufis. At this stage, you think, "Well, that's what it is—I am just the instrument through which God sees." But then you reach another stage when you realize that you are not just the instrument: you *are* His sight. At first you were just the passive instrument; then you realize that in fact it is ridiculous to think that there is God and then there is the instrument. There is only one reality (although there are different stages in this reality). You realize that vision is absolutely unlimited and that your "me" in this is just like a limitation imposed upon an unlimited reality, which you impose because you think you are limited. If you just realize there is no limitation, then there *is* no limitation to the experience. You are carried into the totality of the experience, which is what happens in cosmic consciousness. The person I saw in Hardwar was absolutely cosmic. There are people who you can see are moving about completely closed up in their person, and other people just carry the whole cosmos on their shoulders—they are absolutely cosmic. That is what we should be. That is what we *are*. When we realize this, it is a fantastic discovery. And the consequence is that the one who is aware of the divine perfection becomes a source of tremendous power and light and joy and peace and radiance.

This is why Hazrat Inayat Khan said, "Divinity is human perfection and humanity is divine limitation." It's all one. Things got limited because we have limited them. When you are first able to discover the divine perfection, you can see that it is limited in you and that you are the instrument. But when you realize the divine perfection *in you,* there's no limitation anymore. So one of the practices of the Sufis is to practice the consciousness of the divine perfection.

It is also possible to practice the consciousness of infinity. We think that we are localized in space because the body is localized in space; we think, "I am here, and that other person is there." But Jelal ad-din Rumi says, "This is the greatest wonder, that thou and I, sitting here in the same nook, are at this moment both in Iraq and Khurasan."

We think that we have to be in a certain place because the body is in a certain place. But it is just the body that is in a certain place; you can meet people beyond space. It's just a question of functioning at a different level where there is the experience of spacelessness. The body is a fragment of the earth, and wherever it is in space it has to be localized in space, but there are parts of us that do not have to be localized in space.

Spacelessness is not the same thing as infinity; it means simply not to be in space. Space is just one condition among many other conditions. The practice of spacelessness was recommended by the Buddha among the *arupa jhanas,* which are the contemplations beyond form. When you are able to think of yourself as immaterial or nonsubstantial—that the body is substantial but you yourself are not—then you are able to think of yourself as not localized in space. This is an extraordinary awakening—you see clearly that all the time you were under the impression that you were a personality and a body, and you realize that what happened on the physical plane was purely illusion and that now you are in reality. It is just a question of vantage point.

You have to have courage to doubt the reality of the physical plane, and you have to have courage to believe in the transcendental reality of your being. "Transcendence" is the key word of the New Age, because it moves into further dimensions to attain access to divine intelligence beyond the realms of physical matter and mental constructions. Teilhard de Chardin speaks about the advance of intelligence breaking through matter and forcing its way into other dimensions. We human beings are the spearheads of this forward march because we are somehow able to reach beyond the scaffolding of the body and the mind. We have been all tied up with the mind for all these centuries; we believe in science as an exact knowledge of the mind. Yet the scientists themselves—the more enlightened scientists—have been put in the greatest doubt about the value of the thinking mind.

So we are reaching out into these vaster dimensions. Humanity is becoming conscious of itself as a being. The transformation we see is the passage through a critical stage; one might say that humanity has reached the stage of puberty. There is a new consciousness arising: instead of the segregated consciousness of the parts, there is the consciousness of humanity. From the moment that this consciousness is able to affirm itself, it is able to break through into dimensions of awareness that the individuals cannot reach. Then the individuals participate in the vision of the totality. Something is really happening to humanity, and we have to be gregarious enough, or socially-minded or group-minded enough, to sense what is happening in all of us. Meditation involves us all now; you cannot segregate yourself or isolate yourself in a cell to meditate and reach a certain realization. It's something that is happening to all of us together.

We are reaching into new dimensions of awareness. We have the ability to communicate beyond the physical plane—to reach a person beyond the ocean. The world has become such a small place now: we speak of mass communications. But the communication at the soul level becomes more and more important as time goes on. We *can* fly without wings. And you can become very sensitive, like an aerial, and pick up thoughts; and you can learn how to communicate thoughts and contact beings. Although you may be able to contact them on the mental plane, it is, actually, more difficult: there is a kind of gravity of the mental plane (although it is less heavy than the gravity of the physical plane), whereas higher up there is less substance and therefore less obstruction to the traveling of your soul. That is why you can reach a person's soul more easily than you can reach his mind. So you communicate at the soul level, and then the person whom you have reached has to interpret the impressions he is receiving at the soul level in his mind if he wants to communicate in a concrete way in his thinking and his actions; and it is by this process of osmosis that we are beginning to be aware of it.

You know that a person can really become part of your being—you can begin to think or act like another person, or become so conscious of him that it is as if a part of you became that person. There is a kind of osmosis between people. That is the secret of love, and that is the meaning of love. But you can extend the personal loves that you may have to all beings. For instance, if someone smiles at you on an airplane, that person keeps on living with you for the rest of your life and becomes part of your being. The man I saw in Hardwar has changed my life—and I only saw him for one minute. That is just how powerful one being can be in his effect upon another. And you can extend to incorporate all beings more and more until you become cosmic. You incorporate all the qualities and idiosyncrasies represented by different beings and become very rich and all-comprehensive.

There are several ways of doing this. One is a simple meditation on the starry sky. If you live in a city, your sphere is narrow. You never see a vast horizon unless you live at the top of a skyscraper. But even the physical eyes have a need to look at a distance; in fact, the Tibetans meditate looking into the far distance in the mountains. There is a need in human beings to expand and extend to vast horizons in space and then, beyond that, to let the mind carry us right into the stars and right out into outer space. So instead of being here on the earth and thinking of looking out into outer space, you can think of being in outer space and looking at the earth from that vantage point. You can then apply that to yourself—you can watch yourself walking and think, "Look at that! Isn't that extraordinary? Look at this body walking!" We usually don't realize what a miracle it is that all you have to do is think, "I want to walk," and the body starts walking.

You can also watch your mind from that vantage point, and see that it is following certain laws—it follows a certain pattern, like the thinking of other people. If you watch it happening, you can't be caught up in it anymore. You are able to rise above it and let it happen—without interfering, because nature knows best and the mind has its own working principles; it functions more effectively than it could if you started interfering with it. So you just let it work.

Then, if you watch your emotions arising, you can ask why these emotions arise and think, "Look at me being caught in this trip—just letting myself get caught up in it." If you can watch it, you can't take yourself seriously anymore. You cannot really get angry anymore, except at the times when you become the instrument of the divine wrath—and then it is not your personal anger but something cosmic that is coming through you. It is then that the storm really breaks and clears the atmosphere—and it is wonderful. But even then you could laugh at yourself doing it, because you are not *in* it really; you are just an instrument for this great power. And you can watch yourself being sad or being joyous; you can see how your moods change according to the circumstances and how you are like a puppet in the hands of these emotions.

But when you think of the meaning of it all behind everything, then there is the emotion that lies beyond joy and suffering, and that is ecstasy. Joy has its opposite, which is sorrow; but ecstasy does not have any opposite, because it lies beyond the duality of joy and pain. It comes with the realization of one who is able to watch it all—all the emotions. If you watch the emotions of people—vulgar emotions, sensual emotions, beatific emotions, militant emotions, jubilant emotions, pure emotions or transcendental emotions —you see that each person seems to have a whole gamut of emotions. In one person you find one range of emotions, and in another kind of person you find another range of emotions. Eventually you get to a point where you can "see" where a person is at just by feeling his emotions. There is the person who responds to beauty, and the other person who just walks through it. There is the person who will switch the radio from Bach to hard rock—there's no accounting for taste.

Hazrat Inayat Khan said that everyone has a certain intoxication, his own "wine," and that is the wine that he likes. There might be a person who is just mad about football and who just has to watch it on television or go sit in the rain to watch it. That is his particular kind of madness. We all have our own trips. There was a dervish who was standing in the street laughing his head off, and someone came to him and asked, "What are you laughing about?" The dervish said, "If you could see what I see, you would laugh too." The person said, "I don't see what you see"; and the dervish said, "Well, just look at it! All these people are rushing here and there and they are all intoxicated on their own trips."

The other aspect that we can discover is our timelessness. If you could look upon your life on the earth as an episode in a long series of happenings and recover the memory of the continuity beyond the changes that are the episodes, you would be able to experience yourself as always having been, and as one who will survive the death of your person. The same applies to facing what happened to you before your birth. Do you really believe that you did not exist before you were born? And do you believe that there will be a time when you won't exist? It is completely inconceivable to the soul. So you can discover your immortality if you are able to disidentify yourself with your present personality and consider it just an episode among millions of episodes in the course of your eternal life. Then you identify yourself with that eternal being, which is moving across time and beyond time. You discover yourself in a completely different perspective.

The fear of death is associated with the thought of the annihilation of our personality, because that is what we identify ourselves with. But if you are able to identify yourself with your real being, which is eternal, then there is no fear of transformation or obliteration, because there is a sense of continuity. This gives you another dimension beyond spacelessness—the dimension of timelessness. It gives you a tremendous power: you have come from eternity and carry all the experience of eternity in your being. It has been covered up in the deep layers of the unconscious, so it is difficult to find the memory of it, but it is there; it's just a matter of conviction—knowing that you are an eternal being and carry the whole past, not only of the planet but of the universe, and that you are bringing it out in time. The very narrow framework of time is just forcing the wide dimensions of eternity into this form and space. That is the miracle of life.

Have you ever sat in a room with a person and felt the timelessness of that person? It is as if you were not sitting in that room, but were sitting beyond time and communicating with that person beyond time. Your understanding of that person is quite different than when you are communicating at the personality level. If you are always in your eternal

consciousness, you watch people in their temporal consciousness and think what a pity it is that they cannot see what they
really are in their eternity. And, of course, if you are aware of
your eternal being, you realize that what you thought was
yourself is not yourself. The higher you go, the less specific
you are and the more archetypal you become. You become
more cosmic—the source of timelessness gives you a sense of
the divine perfection. Just as you can experience spacelessness
by looking into the starry sky and thinking of how vast the
universe is, you can look back in history to the Middle Ages
and then to an earlier time and a still earlier time, and you can
think that there is no time when time was not. And yet the
angel at the end of the Apocalypse says, "And time shall be no
more." Time is relative; beyond linear time is another time
that is more cosmic, and there is a time that is still more
eternal beyond that—there are so many different dimensions
of time.

Most of us have a sense of the serenity of one who has
surrounded himself with a zone of silence and is able to walk
on the water, as Christ says—who has the wings of
indifference and detachment, which are "the wings that
enable the soul to fly," as Hazrat Inayat Khan says. These are
the things that give you the ability to walk through life with
great serenity and watch it all and enjoy it. There are phases
you go through, of course. Hazrat Inayat Khan talks about
five phases that lead to this level of development.

In the first phase, you are just like a butterfly; you fly from
flower to flower and you think it is all so wonderful and
beautiful, and you don't feel like taking any responsibility—
you are just enjoying it all. This phase corresponds with youth,
although it is not, of course, dependent upon one's age. Then
you might think, "People are making a fool of me—I should
secure my interests. Look, that person is going ahead, and
that person is going ahead, and I am nowhere. Let me try to

earn some money and have a home," and so forth. And you build up your ego in the rat race. This is the second phase, and a lot of people just remain stuck at that stage—that's where they stay.

But there are those who begin to think, "Well, what's the point? I've got a marvelous home, a marvelous car, and a fine family—and so what? What's the point of it all? I'd like to understand what it is all about—I'd like to pick the toy to bits and see the mechanism of it all." At this stage you develop the need for knowledge and understanding. There is a need for understanding, because people are perplexed by things. They feel that there *must* be a reason. But what good is it just to believe in a reason? You have to really see it. And who is going to show it to you? You go to a teacher in the hope that he will show it, and then, perhaps, you are disappointed because he does not show it to you. He can only point it out to you: that is the whole art of the teacher, to make you turn your head in the direction of what you are supposed to see. He cannot see it for you; he can only point it out to you. You have to see it for yourself. You have to get to a point where you can see, and it is in this phase that we have a need for understanding.

Then you come to the point of detachment. Some people use the word "blasé." You've seen so much, traveled so much —you've seen all of it, and it is always the same—what is the point in traveling anymore? As they say in French, "Plus ça change, plus c'est la même chose"—the more it changes, the more it stays the same. You get to a point where you feel that this is not leading you anywhere, people are so disappointing, and there is nothing to expect of life. A lot of people get to the point where they feel they would just like to retire far away from it all, and maybe in the peace of their solitude discover something. As it is, life is just not particularly interesting anymore. You reach the point where you become an ascetic type. It is better, of course, if this point is reached after you have gone through living intensely; it's very bad to segregate yourself from life because you have had an unhappy love affair or something like that. Many monks and nuns are people who just could not take it and are seeking refuge in protected circumstances. That's not very good, because then if they were exposed again to life, they would probably fail their ideal. It is better to go through it all and then reach the point where you see the value of things, like a child that has grown up and discarded its toys. You've reached the point of higher awareness, you begin to see the value of things, and you begin to realize just how futile are the values that most people are following. What is important to them is not important for you anymore.

The fifth stage is the stage of perfection. Having distanced yourself from life, you come back into life. You can play with the children of the earth and just enjoy it all without any pretence whatsoever—and without any criticism. In the stage of detachment, there is a kind of criticism, or judgment. In the fifth stage there is no judgment any more. You see that people are in the place where they are, everybody is playing his part in the scheme of things and you yourself have your part to play in it all, and it's all a wonderful play. You see beyond it, and you see what it's all about. That is the ideal stage to be in. We can recognize ourselves in all these stages; in fact, it might be more accurate to say that we are all in all these stages at the same time, and sometimes we just have to outline them as stages to make things clearer. We are just like pilgrims advancing on the path—walking without feet and flying without wings and seeing without eyes and hearing without ears. And sometimes we advance, and perhaps sometimes we retrograde. It is not always sure that we are advancing, but two steps forward and one back is better than one step forward and two back. The worst thing that can happen is to develop bitterness because of disappointment.

That's the end—then we've just lost the battle of life. I see so much despair written on the faces of people. They just haven't seen the reason, because it's very difficult to see, and they've given up.

We start out with all the idealism of youth, and then people lose their idealism and think it's just like having believed in Santa Claus. They think, "Now I see reality as it is, and it's not the way I thought." Of course! Your idealism has to be destroyed, just as the idols have to be destroyed. The Tibetans destroy their idols systematically. But your ideals must be replaced by insight. Our ideals are like crutches that we need to start with; then at a certain moment the teacher says, "Do away with your crutches," and then you are left high and dry without any help, like Saint John of the Cross in the dark night of the soul. Saint John said that if you can see, you cannot let yourself be led, because you will say to the one leading you, "No, that is not the right way to go." In order to be led, you have to be blind; and the thing that leads you is your higher intuition in the higher wisdom beyond all things, which you cannot comprehend with your mind. And what you are moving toward is the state Buddha calls "enlightenment," which is the state of all-knowing—and is also the state we should be in right at the beginning of the path. We should be radiant and full of joy, and we should be very peaceful and completely sovereign in all that happens, and we should be just full of love and compassion and understanding for all beings. We know that we should be all these things, and we are looking for them in other beings. That is why people come to spiritual gatherings, and that is why I myself have gone so many times to India. It all arises from the need to discover yourself in a being who is able to manifest to you your real being.

# CHAPTER 11
# Transformation

We have always to consider the application that we make of our meditations: our daily problems. Ideally, we could be in a state of absolute ecstasy while doing the most trivial things or dealing with the most worldly people, without having to detach ourselves. Then we could really share our ecstasy with people, even if they were not attuned to it. Life is like a kind of music—people are attuned to different pitches. For instance, there is a certain atmosphere in the office or in the kitchen or in a coffee house: people get into a certain frame of mind, a certain mood, and then they expect other people to get into their mood. But you bring your world wherever you go. You don't have to get into other people's trips; you can keep on maintaining your attunement. Then it is fantastic what you can do. Instead of running away, which is not helping things, you just keep that attunement. It takes a lot of strength, of course. When you feel that you're depleted, you can just go off somewhere and sit back and meditate until you regain your strength. Then you can start again.

What we are aiming at is the art of being high and of being extremely perspicacious—very clear—while being high. By being "high," we mean not just being euphoric, but being high while having at the same time a tremendous crystal clarity of insight—which is, in fact, wisdom.

You can become, as Hazrat Inayat Khan says, the engineer of the machine. A lot of us are like part of a big machine. It's so big and so overwhelming that we don't know what our part is, let alone see how it functions with relation to all the other parts. Still, we have the choice of being either the machine or the engineer. There's something of the engineer in each one of us: we are the engineer inasmuch as we understand the machine. If our meditation can lead us to the point where we can just see the whole thing very, very clearly, then it has achieved this purpose. If our meditation just leads us away from real things, from tangible things, and takes us into a far-out space somewhere that doesn't have any relationship to everyday life, then it may be very enjoyable, but we're on a trip of our own, not "in the race," as they say. The criterion is to be high—to be in a very high state of consciousness—and be able to look at one's problems, or the problems of other people, without slipping back into one's personal consciousness again.

The focus of people seeking enlightenment has shifted a lot in the course of the last few decades. There was a time when America had discovered Vedanta, and it was a whole new thing. People had been in their churches, and here was a new vision—although they found it a little too theoretical. But then came hatha yoga, which is something you can really work on with your body; and that grew. Then Zen became popular, because people were so fed up with their minds, their opinions, and their theories: Zen came in and blew all that out. The Zen paradox was able to blow the mind, and people found it wonderful.

Then came the drug culture. People were seeking intoxication—seeking to be high. This is a psychological need: one cannot live on bread alone, one also needs wine (I'm misquoting Jesus). There is a certain magic that we really need—otherwise life is so terribly dull. You need that magical thing that just transforms you and everything else—your relationship to people and everything else in your life. That was a good time for Sufism and Sufi dancing—the intoxication of the dervish was very attractive.

Now there is a kind of reaction, embodied in such groups as est. People felt that getting high, on drugs for example, might be wonderful, but then they came down with a bang and didn't know how to relate to their problems. No matter how high you are, it doesn't seem to help you in making decisions or dealing with very material problems. People developed all sorts of psychic disturbances because they were unadapted to the situations that would crop up every day.

And so what we want to do is to use many different techniques so that we can find a way of associating ecstasy with clarity of insight into our problems and other people's problems. So we have to understand how these methods evolved. It's possible that some methods applied to a certain situation at a certain time in history, and now we have to look upon them in a different vein. For example, with *kundalini* yoga you can transform the functions of the body to such a degree that you enter into a state of hibernation: you get into the anabolic state as opposed to the catabolic state. This means that energy is going to be maintained, and you can actually combine a state of deep sleep with awakening. This condition is wonderful for rishis who leave the world and go and sit in the Himalayas in the snow, with no means of eating at all. They go for years and years without any food at all, and obviously it is only possible to do this by bringing about a transformation of the functions of the body and the whole metabolism of the body. The heartbeat is slowed, the blood pressure and body temperature are lowered. The consequence is an extraordinary intuition that people in ordinary life are unable to develop. These rishis can see right into the detail of a person's life. There is a power in their glance that cannot possibly be developed in one who is continually subjected to the impressions of everyday life. The peace of those beings, and the power, are very, very rare.

Of course, it would be wonderful if we could develop that while being in the middle of everyday life. But the whole orientation of those meditations is away from the creative realm. Physical reality falls out of focus. According to a text of the Hindus, "Physical reality is a condition of reality"—and that means *a* condition of reality in the same sense that ice is *a* condition of water. I've often spoken to rishis in their caves, and I could see that they had to make a real effort to come down—to focus themselves in the physical plane, and even to understand what I was saying, because I was speaking from the point of view of one who was conscious of physical reality while they were not conscious of physical reality at that time.

When I was myself meditating with the rishis and got into the same consciousness they were in, then I could communicate with them in a completely different way. They didn't have to bring their consciousness down to the physical plane. This seems to be a prototype of meditation from which we can learn, because that's the way that meditation has been presented in its classical form. But living in the world, we have to find a way of doing precisely the opposite: instead of cutting ourselves away from physical reality, we want to be able to be conscious in our higher consciousness and at the same time function from the physical plane, seeing physical reality in its relativity without letting it draw us down into its limitation.

For example, if you are able to look at a flower and realize that it is the crystallization of vibrations that have their existence in the *akashic* plane, the world of archetypes, then you are not limited by the physical flower that you see there, because you have a total experience. Or, when you meet a person, instead of being caught in the personality of the person or the physical appearance of the person, you could see the total reality of that person, and there would be no comparison in the magnitude of your experience. This is what we are aiming at.

It's not without reason that what Hazrat Inayat Khan calls "the Message of our time" seems to have been born of Sufism, because this is precisely the attitude of the dervish. He is intoxicated to such a point that he's like a drunken man. He's so absolutely gone in his consciousness—and at the same time he's continually with beings and involving himself in their lives and trying to bring them this other dimension, instead of retiring away from the haunts of men.

One kind of practice that is very useful for extending consciousness involves the use of themes—something to have your thoughts upon. You can begin with simple concentrations on a circle and a square and progress to something sophisticated like a crystal or a sphere, then go on to a much more sophisticated one like the drops of water on the surface of a lake or a stream of water in the middle of a kind of frozen, frigid landscape of the soul. You start with more tangible themes and progress to themes that are unearthly, that correspond to dreams, and you get deeper and deeper into higher strata of consciousness. You start with concentrations: you are there and the object is there in front of you, and you're still down in the ordinary state most people are in—in duality, as they call it in Hinduism. Then you gradually get into the object, so that you identify yourself with the object, and get right into it. You experience a depth that you can't when you consider the object as other than yourself.

In fact, you bring about a transformation of your

consciousness, extending consciousness from its limitation by its localization in the person into wider and wider spheres outside the immediate environment—right out into the spheres of beings. You can go right into the conciousness of the angelic beings; the angelic sphere is consigned somewhere to the memory of our unconscious, but most people just cut it all out. They've gotten right down into the immediate environment and closed themselves in it and forgotten all about all the horizons we have crossed over on our way down—all the landscapes, all the worlds, and all the reality that we have been through and are still in communication with. We simply limit ourselves to the immediate environment and divorce ourselves from the higher spheres.

You can go beyond the realm of forms and images to the archetypes. This can get difficult—although it is not really difficult—because people are not used to it. They have difficulty in dealing with attributes, or archetypes, such as rosehood, for example, or the archetype of your being. We're used to dealing with concrete things, like personalities. As soon as we start reaching beyond the concrete, it seems unreal. But unless we can do that, we can't ever understand and see physical reality in all its dimensions, because we get limited in the physical object. And yet we carry the archetypes of all things in our own consciousness, in the collective unconscious. We carry the inheritance of all levels of reality in our very blood, incorporated right down into the flesh.

For example, you do not only inherit in your body the bodies of your parents: the cells of your body are the very cells of the bodies of your parents that have conjugated. It's not another body; it's the proliferation of those very cells. And we carry in our bodies not only the bodies of our parents, but of all the ancestors right back into the whole past of the planet— the dinosaurs, the fish, the rocks, and everything. The interfusion of spirit and matter in our flesh is an extraordinary thing. You can't really say that your body is just your body and not really you—it does incorporate your being, because of that interfusion. A better word than "interfusion," actually, is "transfusion." An interfusion is a mixture: an interfusion of earth and water would be mud. Transfusion means that physical matter is penetrated by something that we call "spirit" and that brings it to life. We carry right down into our body not only the physical inheritance of our parents and all our ancestors, but the inheritance of the personalities not only of our ancestors but also of all the beings in the higher planes, like the angels, the djinns, and the archangels—right up to the very top, which Hazrat Inayat Khan calls our "divine inheritance." This is why he said that Christ was perfectly entitled to call himself the Son of God—because he was aware of his divine inheritance. This is what it's all about: being able to make functional an inheritance that is recessive in the sense in which the word is used in biology—latent and not yet active. We can see the development of recessive characteristics even in plants; for example, there is the possibility of a blue rose in a red rose, but it's recessive, it's latent, and if you bring about certain transformations, the blueness will come out. As it is, it has been overcome by the redness.

So all the qualities are there, and through meditation we can bring them out. We say that this transforms a person, but you can't really transform a person—you can only make him what he really already is by making him conscious of what he already is. Meditation is just that: it is making people conscious of what they are. And in order to become what one is, one has to see what one is in another oneself. That is the reason for all the communications of beings: you become like the beings whom you see. You really already are them, but it hasn't become manifest yet. And you can imagine the joy of the heavens—just that wonderful experience of being in communication with wonderful beings, the ecstasy of being in the presence of wonderful beings. That's the real meaning of love. It's being absolutely blown away by the being of a person who intoxicates you because that person manifests the thing you long for, which is the object of your nostalgia, which is what we mean by God—the One we all love. I'm very discreet about using the word "God," because people immediately think it's getting very dogmatic. Most of us don't know it, but it's that reality, that Being whom we love. And this is the essence of Sufism—the One you love.

There are other practices that do not use a theme. One of the best of these is *nidra* yoga. In samadhi, we use themes and gradually internalize them, and we tutor consciousness into surviving the destruction of its scaffolding so that consciousness is able to continue to function while we take away from it what it used to hold on to. We keep on taking those themes away. If you're not careful and you overdo it, consciousness sinks into a trance state if you don't keep feeding it with something that will hold it and keep it active. But we make those themes more and more subtle and keep consciousness burning bright while we take away its support, and then get the support more and more fine, until there's no support. That is deep sleep—there's no support: no thoughts, no emotions, absolutely nothing but pure consciousness. Most people sink in that state into deep sleep, but if you can avoid sinking, and you keep your consciousness high and bright, that is the technique of *nidra* yoga. This is what is meant by awakening. You can enter a room and be absolutely awake, and feel that everybody is caught up in something or other but that you've awakened from the place where they are. That's illumination. When a person speaks, you can see from where his speaking comes. He's still in the place where he sees things in a limited way.

Of course, when you come across a person who is awake and you're still slumbering, you can't remain indifferent to him.

Somehow he does something to you. He awakens you by his awakening; in the light of his being, you can see what you couldn't see otherwise. The work of all the spiritual masters in the past has been just that—to awaken people who, as Hazrat Inayat Khan says, are "turning over in their sleep." If they're happy where they are, then there's no hurry. But if they're unhappy in the place where they are, then it's good to help them.

The difference between *nidra* yoga and samadhi is that in *nidra* yoga we don't use themes that are set. You just let the spontaneity of your being project pictures if necessary, and if it doesn't feel like projecting pictures, it doesn't. Your crutches can be a handicap: they can really limit you. You prefigure your meditation by deciding that you are going to take this or that theme, and by so doing you give a definite slant and a definite limitation to your consciousness. On the other hand, if people are just going to sit there and start regurgitating all the impressions of the mind and try to fight against their thoughts, that is not meditation. In that case it is much better to use a theme. But you might give yourself a theme and then, at a certain moment, get right down into that deep place where there are absolutely no projections, no outer things, no *prakriti*. Still, this is only half the battle. It's wonderful for everyone to get right down into the depths of his being sometimes, and to feel life sprouting from the depths— the very energy of life in its purity, like a source of water that is gurgling from the earth. It's important. But what do you do with it?

For instance, transcendental meditation is very nice; people are busy, and it's nice to take some time to get down into that deep place within yourself and to relax. It's very useful, and it plays a very important part in our time. But what we're trying to do is to get to a place where we can see the whole purpose of everything around us. Then we can see the cause behind the cause behind the cause, as Murshid says. We can feel the pulsing of the universe and see the purpose toward which all men are striving. And that, of course, is a far greater thing.

When you get high, you can do practices with magnetism, because that is the moment when you develop a lot of power and when it is good to apply that power and give it a channel outward. I don't think it's good when the power accumulates; it is better not to keep it all within yourself. So when it begins to develop, that is the moment to place the hands forward so that the energy is radiated out. That is also the moment to experience the radiation of your aura and the radiation of your *akashic* or vibratory body.

Scientists are now measuring the field of the aura and the influence of thought on the aura. They have found that simply by thinking of light, people can make their auras burn more brightly. Many people think it's just imagination to think about light, but the fact is that imagination is very creative. If you just think about light, your aura begins to burn more brightly.

Then you might go into the *dhikr* dance of the Sufis, which is the same thing as the whirling of the planets and the dance of Shiva. It's ecstasy, of course; it's a kind of wine. It's not all the wine there is, it's just a certain kind of wine. As humanity moves forward—and we can think of humanity as continually evolving—we are continually breaking into new horizons of emotion. Not just new realizations, but new horizons of emotion. The *dhikr* dance opens us up to planetary emotion, instead of the emotion of the individual. It's part of what is called group consciousness. You become part of the group that is getting into a certain attunement. When you move, you are the energy that causes you to move: it's not your own energy, but the energy of the group that you are focalizing in your particular person. This is a completely different dimension of meditation, because you're not sitting alone and isolating yourself in your meditation, but are participating in the whole group. The group itself is, of course, reflecting the feeling of the planets—of the galaxies, in fact—and in that sense it's a cosmic experience, particularly as it is related to the process of dying and rising from one's death, or resurrecting.

This experience contrasts with samadhi, which is getting into your higher consciousness and overcoming any sense of the self. In the *dhikr*, you are annihilated by the divine operation upon you. You don't annihilate yourself; you let yourself *be* annihilated. There is always, in Sufism, the consciousness of the action of God upon one, instead of doing things oneself. That is why the Sufi always says, "I'm so shattered by what I see. I'm so overwhelmed." Of course, he then goes on to say that it is God who is shattered in him.

We begin by thinking, "I'm looking for the divine Beloved." But very soon, the whole order of things is changed, and we say, "I'm experiencing God in me," or "I'm experiencing God shattering me." There's always the sense of that overwhelming consciousness. The difference between that and samadhi is that Sufism represents a stage in the consciousness of humanity where God became more personal. It's not that our *concepts* of God have become more personal; it's because there's a change in the divine Being. As we incarnate more—and, in the West, people have become more incarnated than in the East—we become more attuned to physical matter and more able to master matter. There is a change in the divine consciousness that becomes a person. The mystery of God becoming a person is intangible; if you tried to make a theory of it, it would just be intellectual. But there is the consciousness of the Presence here, not out there—it is not a matter of dissolving yourself in outer space. You become conscious of the Presence right here, in your midst. Al-Hallaj was crucified when he said, "Ana'-l Haqq"

—"I am the truth"—by which is meant that that which says "I" in me is God. He was accused of having revealed the secret of his relationship with God, which was his awareness of the presence of God as being right there with him.

This leads us very far into something that is very important for us to understand in our time. It's important because we're exposed to so many different teachers, and each teacher teaches something different. It gets really very confused; you think, "Whom am I to follow?" Each teacher teaches something that has a tremendous value, and yet they're all different. A swami comes and teaches about *shakti* energy, and then a Sufi dervish comes and leads you into a far-out dervish dance, and then there are Zen teachers and so many others. The Theravada Buddhism is so different from the Tantra of the Tibetans. There are so many different ways, and we can value all these ways, but it is important for us to see how they all dovetail—how they fit together. That is what's important in this process: understanding the whole picture and how it affects us.

We don't have conflicts in our being, but we're almost forced to the comparison because so many teachers are here. Samadhi will bring you into the dissolution of the focal center of your consciousness and thence into total consciousness, so that there is absolutely no consciousness of the person. If a fly moves on your head, you don't twitch; and if someone calls you, even by your name, you don't hear. Personal consciousness has been totally eradicated. This leads to liberation—but liberation from what? Many people think it means liberation from the necessity of coming down to the earth again; in any case, it's liberation from the personal consciousness.

The other extreme is the sense of incarnation. In Christianity, for example, there is the incarnate God. This polarization reaches its fullness in the words of Abu Yazid al-Bistami, the great Sufi hermit of the ninth century. He was immersed in the typical Sufi practice of incorporating the divine qualities so that one becomes the manifestation of God on earth. Bistami said, "God said to me, 'O Abu Yazid, verily My creatures long to see thee,' and I said, 'Adorn me with Thy unity and clothe me with Thy I-ness and raise me up in Thy oneness, so that when Thy creatures see me, they may say, "We have seen Thee and Thou art that." Yet I (Abu Yazid) will not be there at all.'" That is the meaning of *fana*—the annihilation of the self. But it is exactly the opposite of samadhi, because it gives importance to the human vehicle as a means whereby the abstract can become concrete. In samadhi, you're getting into the abstract and away from the concrete. In the *fana* state, there is a sense of the reality of God as a person, whereas in the samadhi perspective, God is all: it's not concrete, it's beyond creation. God is transcendent. In the *fana* dimension, God is immanent. That is why Sufis speak about the presence of the Beloved.

This is epitomized by the words of Farid ad-din Attar, when he says, "Renounce the good of the world, renounce the good of heaven, renounce your highest ideal, and then renounce renunciation." You follow the path of liberation; you're nearly there—you could be free from all this—and you meet the great challenge: to give up your liberation out of love. That's the challenge of our time, and that is why it is important to see how all these practices dovetail, and what their relevance is. If you can't get right out into samadhi, you might perhaps get too caught up in your problems and not be able to see them in perspective. You have to be able to lift yourself up to see them. Then you liberate yourself. When you are annihilated by the divine action, God is experienced as a person by the fact that He operates on you. There's a definite action, which is where there's a feeling of relationship. Otherwise, you are God, and then there's no dichotomy.

The alchemists of the Middle Ages were discovering the process of transformation. When you know the secret of the stages you go through in transformation, you understand what's happening to you. Something that happens to a lot of people in our time is the disintegration of personality. It's a very frightening thing, and people often go to a psychiatrist and think there is something very wrong with them. In fact, this disintegration is part of the process of transformation: you can't progress unless you disintegrate and are rebuilt again. An intelligent psychiatrist really provides for the continuity of a person's being in the middle of the disruption of the elements of his being. It's a question of earmarking the principle of your being and hanging on to the principle while all the contingency begins to scatter. If you let the principle of your being scatter, you're lost. This is what the alchemists describe when they say, "The red lion with wings, the winged lion gets lost." If you're distilling chemicals and they evaporate, you've lost your chemicals. You have to be able to hold the red lion, which is the volatile condition of matter— the subtle part of your being, the essence or quintessence or principle of your being. You have to hang on to the principle of your being; otherwise you experience what is called insanity, which is a process of transformation that has gone wrong because it wasn't properly supervised.

In that sense, we all exemplify very typical cases of insanity —at least, I hope we do, because there's nothing more boring than a normal person. Of course, you can promote that dissolution, providing you know where you are going: you have to be very careful playing about with a human being, because it's a very subtle mechanism. But since life will break you down anyway, it's sometimes better for you to do it yourself. That's what the dervish does: his personality is just gone. The personality is something that we hang on to because it's wonderful to have a lot of charm. You can count upon your charm. And when you've lost your charm, you feel you haven't got anything to hang on to anymore. But it is then that you become real, because your charm was just a veneer. It's a matter of becoming more and more real.

Just imagine the richness of our being! That richness is being hampered by the fact that we hang on to the crystallization of it in our personality. Our being has become fossilized in the personality—or at least a part of our being or a projection of our being has become fossilized in the personality. And people hang on to their personality like grim death. They hope people will like them for their personality, when in fact they're much more than that. But then something in life happens and you go to pieces; your personality goes to pieces. The best thing that can happen to you then is to become conscious of what you are, because otherwise you're nowhere. The principle of this process is *solve et coagula*— dissolve and rebuild again. It's a rebirth, and to experience it you have to go through the process of dissolution.

So the first process you go through is simply dissolution, which can reach a point of terrible darkness—what Saint John of the Cross called "the dark night of the soul." His case is typical of someone who went through it right to the very end. Another typical person is Abu Yazid al-Bistami, who said, "I reached the threshold of non-being and soared within it for ten years, passing from denial to denial through denial . . . . Then I attained the reaches of deprivation, the threshold of union, and soared within it by dint of denial in utter destitution until I was bereft of deprivation in my abandonment and was deprived even of my destitution by the sheer denial of denial and the deprivation of deprivation." Of course, his language is not logical at all—he was just trying to convey this sense of deprivation. He used the word *kemal,* which is the nothingness you go through.

Saint John of the Cross said that, for example, you might be meditating and experiencing what he calls "delight"—the delight of the presence of God—when all of a sudden you're blank. Nothing happens. And you find yourself completely miserable in your being, and you feel so inadequate. This is because you're hanging on to this thing that hasn't become real enough in your being and has therefore been taken away. He goes on to say that you go through the real dark night of the understanding, where it's not the personality that dissolves, but you feel that everything you've ever believed in is nonsense. It's no good trying to work it out in your mind, because it's not a good enough computer to be able to understand things. People build their lives on certain opinions, and they're so convinced of those opinions. When they suddenly realize that those opinions are not valid, they crumble. The whole mind crumbles. And they think it's a terrible thing, but it's the best thing that could happen— much better than hanging on to things that aren't real.

Of course, you really do go through a very deep trip; and the worst thing is that it affects your belief, because your thoughts give substance to your belief. If those thoughts crumble, then you don't know what to believe in anymore. The real crisis is at that level. It's not so much a question of believing or not believing in God; that's the concept of the mind. It's a question of believing that things make sense. In that sense, every scientist is a believer, because he assumes that things make sense; otherwise, he wouldn't be able to find out what sense there is. The real crisis—the darkest part of the night, which Saint John of the Cross calls "the middle of the night"—comes when you're desperately fighting to hold on to faith in the middle of the darkness. And, believe me, it is only that faith that will carry you through the night. You can call that faith the belief in the impossible possibility—believing in spite of proof of the opposite. A weak being relies upon evidence for what he believes, and a strong being has the power to maintain his belief even while the mind nullifies what he knows in his intuition. You're tested in that when you're facing a person and that person tells you something that seems true enough; you can't question it; and yet you're looking into his soul and you know that he is lying. You don't allow the evidence of the mind to take away your intuition of what you know: that's the real test.

That's what Saint John of the Cross was going through. He went through it, with his tremendous faith, when everything was breaking down. And this act of faith represents a second stage in the alchemical process. We call it hanging on to the essence while letting go of the contingency. In the process of resurrection, the essence of our being is extracted from all the different aspects of our being. Once that essence has been extracted, then it doesn't matter if the rest of the being is dissolved, because that extract is the most important thing. When the perfume, which is the essence of the flower, has been extracted from the flower, the rest can be thrown away—that's the contingency.

So you become conscious of the essence of your being, and that is the only safety in insanity. That is the cure, in fact—that we can make a person conscious of his real being. Then even if his apparent being breaks down, he is able to survive. If you don't give him that, he sinks. If you look upon your personality as a continuity in change and then reach into the consciousness of what you have always been, beyond all change, that is the essence of your being. That is what we do in the practice of samadhi, and it is the second stage. The Greeks put their initiates through that same practice in the Eleusinian mysteries, and they called the second stage the "rise of Apollo." There's something very optimistic about that, like the sun rising again. A new awareness comes out of the breaking down, as Hazrat Inayat Khan says—"Out of the shell of the broken heart emerges the newborn soul." So the practices of the second stage consist of identifying yourself with pure consciousness, for example, and considering your body, or your mind, as the vehicle of consciousness. You identify yourself with the very essence of your being.

That process is carried still further in the third stage, which can only be described as the stage in which you really identify with the Absolute—the pure essence of your being. It is sometimes called the "immaculate state." It's like the alchemical process that led to the formation of the philosophers' stone; it is the quintessence, the feeling of being ethereal. It is like being the butterfly that emerges out of the cocoon. The state of nirvana in Buddhism corresponds most closely to this third stage. You get to the source of life, beyond all forms. Samadhi leads to that, of course, which is why samadhi is so important: it brings you up to the third stage, which is represented by the Virgin Mary, the crescent moon, the immaculate state, Elijah, and the water of life. It is the stage of aloofness and detachment—peace, instead of joy.

Then you go through the fourth stage, which is coming down again. This is the end of the *solve*—the dissolution. It marks the beginning of the second phase, which is incarnation, or *coagula*—the process of re-formation. You experience your rebirth, and by experiencing it, you participate willfully and intentionally in your rebirth. This is how evolution takes place.

In our rebirth, two processes are present. These two processes are epitomized by the two serpents in the symbol of the caduceus—the two forces of life that are continually interpenetrating and crisscrossing one another. Sometimes life goes more towards the coagulation state, and at other times it tends more towards dissolution.

When a person is pure spirit, you can't hold him—he's not coagulated. If a person gets fossilized—as many people do—he becomes stereotyped, and only an infusion can transform him. In the alchemical process, you are subjecting yourself to an intense current of life that is going to renew you totally, and you have to identify with that current. That's the moment at which you feel, "I'm pure spirit." On the other hand, you are conscious of the forms through which the spirit is working. In fact, birth is the encounter of all that descends from heaven and all that ascends from the earth. At that moment, all the inheritance you have from the angels, from all of your life in the higher spheres, makes contact with all that has happened on the earth since the beginning of time. You can think of yourself as a visitor from outer space who has landed on the planet and is using the substance of the planet to work with the conditions of the planet. That's what birth is: the moment when there's a contact between your having always been, with all the inheritance that you've brought, and the planet Earth. You are infusing the planet Earth with what you're bringing down from your soul, and when you leave after death, you have left a mark on the planet. One might say that for the planet Earth to be able to unfold, it has had to draw into itself all that has accrued to it from the higher planes.

For example, for a plant to become a plant—to grow—it has had to draw the earth into itself and make a plant out of the earth. It has drawn the air into itself and made a plant out of the air. It has drawn the sun into itself and made the sun into a plant. It has drawn the stars into itself and made the stars into a plant. It has drawn the angels into itself and made the angels into a plant.

So you can experience the miracle of birth. And by experiencing it, you are able to do it consciously—you consciously incorporate the heavens into your being, and you consciously incorporate the earth into your being. You create that integration out of your own free will—because the greatest gift of God is our free will. At that moment, you become conscious of being the angels incorporated, and you are conscious of being the earth and all the other elements, instead of being conscious of just being your personality.

When that happens, you're a new person. Of course, people still have their picture of you as they remember you. When Buddha came down, his five disciples, who had left him and had not seen him for a long time, decided to go and see what he was like. And Buddha said to them, "Have I ever spoken to you thus before?" He said this not because he was on an ego trip, but because he wanted them to know that they mustn't consider him as he was before, because he had become another person. There is a proverb that says a prophet is without honor in his own country, and this is because people hold you down into the image that you have made of yourself. So when you have undergone a transformation, you have to affirm your being; unless you can affirm it, people will bring you right back to where you were before. That is why the fifth stage is the affirmation of your being, when you face the temptation to follow the easier path and just fall back into your personality.

It's really very difficult to be your being. It's so much easier to say, "Well, you know, I'm just this imperfect being. I have these habits, and you just have to take me as I am." Everybody does that, but that's not the spiritual way. It is true that the spiritual way is the way of humility, but you have to be truthful in your humility—you have to affirm the reality of what you represent. It's not an ego trip, it's what you really are. You mustn't let people limit you to your personality, and you mustn't rest in your personality. You can get very high, but if when you come down you get right back into your personality, everything is lost. So the fifth stage is the affirmation of your real self.

Then you get to the sixth stage, which is the end of the process; it is expressed in the formula, "the spiritualization of matter and the materialization of spirit." You are conscious of being spirit that is experiencing matter, and you are conscious of being matter that is experiencing spirit; and so matter is transformed by spirit and spirit is transformed by matter. The human being is the perfect balance between these two. Then you realize, of course, the whole significance of your life. It is a very great realization to understand the stages that we actually go through in our life—and that we can promote them.

The meditations for the New Age correspond to the last stage, which is experiencing the spirit while you're dealing with matter, instead of just going up into spirit, which is the third stage. This is why the first three stages—the first phase—are called the "minor mysteries," while the last three stages—the second phase—are called the "major mysteries." We could generalize—without forgetting that it is unfair to generalize—that samadhi or nirvana is the minor mystery, because it gets you to the third stage where you're just pure spirit and have gone beyond life; and the esoteric teachings of Judaism and Islam correspond to the major mystery, bringing spirit down into matter.

For those who are interested in astrology, the six phases are also said to correspond to particular planets. The first stage corresponds to Saturn, which is symbolized by a crescent moon below a cross. The second phase corresponds to Jupiter, which is the crescent moon above the cross. The third phase is the crescent moon, which expresses the receptive quality of womanhood—which is why there is the image of the Virgin Mary standing on the crescent moon. The crescent moon always represents the responsive, receptive attitude of the one who has become totally selfless in the third stage. So the minor mysteries consist in the rising of the moon. The major mysteries correspond to the sun and the descent of the sun. The fourth phase corresponds to Venus, which is the rebirth or holy marriage—the alchemical betrothal—and is symbolized by the sun above the cross. The next phase corresponds to Mars, which is shown by the sun underneath the cross. Finally, there is just the sun: the last phase is the solar phase, when man is the Christ being. It is typified by the alchemists' gold, which is the end of the whole process.

At the end of the process, you become adamant, just as gold is adamant; you can't be changed anymore. At the beginning of the process you had to go through a change, and at the end of the process you have become coagulated. You have re-formed in such a way that you cannot be dissolved anymore. But, of course, it may be that you go through another cycle. You may repeat the whole cycle again.

# CHAPTER 12

# The Sacredness of Life

What do we mean by spirituality? Do we mean adherence to a set of rules or dogma, or a devotional attitude towards the guru, or a rather sanctimonious and unreal emotion that does not have to do with life? Obviously not. It's not in a series of beliefs or dogma or lip service to something that is at loggerheads with what one is doing in practice. There are those who believe that it is good enough just to be good—to practice right conduct and action and be totally honest and fair to people. But spirituality is much more than all that.

Without trying to go into big definitions and discussions of things in actual practice, we might say first that spirituality manifests most tangibly in how we deal with problems, especially in relationships with people; secondly, in whether we unfold the potentialities in our being and how we unfold them; and finally, in absolute crystal-clear understanding of what lies behind the appearance of things—not being caught up in the appearance but really seeing the "cause behind the cause and the purpose beyond the purpose." It should lead to an extraordinary clarity that should give a great brilliance to your whole being: your consciousness can become like a light that illuminates all things, and you yourself can become like a crystal—absolutely clear.

As far as relationships with people go, it should be very clear that you cannot see things clearly if you are always judging things from your own vantage point—"This person has been unfair to me and this person is just like a stick in my wheels, and this person drags me down, and this person inspires me," and so on. These are all personal opinions, deriving from the fact that you are looking at things from your own vantage point. So the first thing you have to do is apply the principle of meditation and de-center your consciousness from the very narrow vantage point of the person, and just try to experience what things look like from the point of view of the other—especially the person you have a grudge against. Maybe his point of view is narrow, just like yours, but at least you will have completed your vantage point by his. It won't give you total insight, but if you can complete it by the transcendental insight that is looking at the cause behind the cause, you will begin to see things very clearly. Then you begin to see motivation—both what is motivating you to take the attitude you have towards him and what is motivating him. Finally you look to see what is the divine programming behind the whole thing—what do you have to learn from it all? Then you can really make something out of the situation, rather than just deploring it and finding that it's obstructive to your life or your unfoldment.

Then you realize that everything is just wonderful. What seems to be a problem is really a wonderful challenge, and what seems to be a failure avers itself to be a success. And sometimes when you think you have gained something over a person or that you have sustained a success, in fact it avers itself to be a loss, a defeat. Things are very different from the way they appear. You might want something from someone and then look back ten years later and think how lucky it is that what you wished for in your relationship never happened —or what a pity that it did. You realize that you're caught in a certain perspective. So you could say that spirituality is freeing yourself from a narrow perspective that you get into because of the conditioning of the environment or the circumstances of your life. It's a wonderful feeling to be free from your preconceived ideas and from the perspective of your emotions, which alter from one moment to the next. The consequence is that you are free from two things, the sense of a heavy conscience and the sense of a grudge—and this freedom is the sine qua non of the conditions of any spiritual development.

Hazrat Inayat Khan discusses these two things in his book *The Inner Life.* In dealing with the conscience, you want to be quite sure that there is no person with whom you are dealing unjustly. So first of all you have to be very clear in your mind—in your realization—as to those people with whom you have dealt unfairly or to whom you owe a debt, not necessarily of money but of good will or whatever else you might feel you owe them. Sometimes we just refuse to recognize our fault because we're afraid of losing face, or that the person will consider our acknowledgement a weakness and will take advantage of it. But sometimes it's a question of our own ego: we don't want to admit that we did wrong, and so we just bury our intuition of having been wrong from our sight, and then we have to live with a conscience that is somehow bugging us from under the cover of the unconscious, and which is a kind of poison. You can't dance with joy as long as there's a feeling of having been unfair to someone. You might say there's nothing much you can do about it, but perhaps you could still write to the person; if not, the fact of your recognition of the debt is already something. The best thing you can do, of course, is to decide that you're going to do just anything—you can never compensate for the wrong you've done, but you're prepared to do anything for people, if for no other reason than because there is a debt owed somehow to the world.

The other problem is the feeling that you've been unfairly dealt with by someone else. You bear a grudge, and that grudge is a poison. You can never dance with joy as long as you feel that you've been badly treated by that person. The best thing to do in this case is to consider that person the stick with which God hit you, just like the Zen master: it was really for your good. But the trouble is that there is a tendency to displace the problem: people have a secret grudge against destiny, which is really God; "destiny" is just a polite way of saying God. That is a very serious wound. You can never dance with joy if you feel like that, and it also stands in the way of your unfoldment. So it is something you really have to face and come to terms with; you have to realize that it is impossible for our judgment or our understanding totally to encompass the programming behind things. There has to be an act of faith to realize that there is some meaning behind the problem that you might not see, but that you could do something about if you could see it. For example you might be tested in your compassion or your ability to stand by your ideal or to master yourself. You can only use your intuition to find out the quality the situation is trying to make you develop, but then you could make something positive out of it instead of just deploring the situation—in which case you've lost the chance to make good from it and, what is more, you've developed bitterness. That is one thing we must be very careful about—the bitterness we nurture in ourselves.

In our community, the Abode of the Message, we had a kind of policy that if anyone had a grudge against anyone else, he should just go to that person and deal with it openly. If this is done as a matter of course, it is taken for granted and people aren't offended about it. And if you can talk about it without getting all up tight or angry, it's wonderful, because it releases a lot of things and perhaps people can explain things that they didn't realize needed explaining. There is a chance for understanding and perhaps admitting that one has made a mistake. We're all fallible. It's better to lose face than to lose faith: no one can take away what you are or give you what you're not, so acknowledging what is wrong will not diminish you in any way. In fact, it will make you much more appreciated for being totally honest with yourself and other people.

It is very important to realize what you are doing to people. Are you inspiring people, or are you loading all your woes onto them—or do you just meet them like ships in the night, very superficially? Just imagine the tremendous opportunity that the encounter of two people offers: the chance to discover yourselves in each other, to fulfill yourselves by seeing that which in you is simply a latency, and to become that which has not yet manifested in you by seeing it in another person. It's a wonderful opportunity. But if you are judgmental, then you are criticizing instead of exchanging or sharing; and, of course, the thing that kills relationship is criticism. We are endowed with our own discrimination, and we have to use it. We can't approve of everything—as long as we know our opinion is relative. But there is a way of criticizing that is constructive and a way that is negative, and very often a problem arises because we would like a person to be the way we want that person to be, and we have no right to do this. We have to love the person and value the person for the way he or she is. Of course, it goes much deeper than that, because somewhere in our intuition we are able to see the perfect nature of the person. His personality is a very imperfect manifestation of his perfect being, and so while our judgment is seeing the imperfect aspect of his being, our intuition sees the perfect aspect. The image that is seen by our intuition is hurt by witnessing qualities or defects in the person that are exactly the opposite of what we know to be the real person. We tend to forget about our intuition and just judge the person, but if you could never lose sight of your real intuition of the wonderful qualities of the person, then you could criticize in a constructive way, without giving offense.

This is especially important, of course, when there is a very great love between people. For example, if your children know that you love them, you can reprimand them, as long as it's not done with hatred but with the purpose of teaching them things that they don't realize yet. Children get very insecure if they're allowed to do everything. They want to know exactly where the limits are, and they like to be disciplined. It gives a child a sense of security. The same thing is true of grown people. People will sometimes try things on you, and it's better if you let them know from the beginning where the frontier is: that's where it's at, they can't go beyond that. People will respect you for it, and there can be a very loving relationship when they know that that's the lie of the land. And the more you love people and the more they know you love them, the more you can perhaps allow yourself to say how you wish they could really be what they are, really be manifested. It's like a music teacher telling a student how to play better and to do better than he or she is doing; otherwise the student would never progress. That's positive criticism.

The worst thing you can do to people is to undermine their self-esteem. People are very touchy when it comes to being criticized insofar as they identify themselves with their personality: if you criticize their personality, then of course you make them lose their sense of self-esteem, which is sometimes the most sensitive part of the whole being. Ibn al-'Arabi says that as an artist doesn't like your criticizing his painting, so God is offended by your criticizing any creature. There is a sense of sacredness behind this that is very important, quite apart from love: perhaps it's the depths of love. If you have a great respect for the sacredness of a being, you open up a door of communication at a very deep level, because you consider that person sacred; that person is like a sacred charge to you. In the marriage ceremony, we ask if you will regard the other person as your most sacred charge. In this case it's particularly strong, but all people are something very sacred that you carry in your soul, and they have to be safe in your keeping.

In fact, this is the basis of friendship: when you know that there is a person you can talk to, that's friendship. You can't talk to all people because, first of all, there are those who would probably laugh at you and treat you with derision. There are certain things you don't feel like opening up to people about because they might not value them. The second thing in friendship is that you want to know that the people you trust will value the secrecy of what you convey to them. You can open up very innocently about what you feel, but that doesn't mean you would want to say it to everybody; and if a person in whom you've confided says it to someone else, you've been betrayed. Thirdly, you want to know that your friend will value your highest ideal—not just understand it, but really value it. That's why you can't open your soul to people who would have no idea what you're talking about or of what is so meaningful for you. Behind it all is the feeling that this person has a sense of sacredness. Betrayal is always related to sacredness, because betrayal is always defiling something that is sacred. This is the depth of spiritual life: a feeling of sacredness. That is what one really means by God.

CHAPTER 13

# Discovering the Order
# Behind the Universe

Sufism is about the least definable thing there is—and, of course, people are always asking, "What is Sufism?" In fact, the "ism" doesn't belong there, and "Sufi" is about the last thing you would ever call yourself: it means "woolly," and nobody would call him- or herself "woolly." It comes from a conversation between a dervish and a mullah, who represents the orthodoxy of Islam, in the eighth century. The mullah reprimanded the dervish for wearing wool; he should have been wearing cotton, because the Prophet wore cotton and he should follow the example of the Prophet. The dervish replied, "I am following the tradition of Jesus." In those days, the Arabs knew very little about Christianity, but they knew something about Christian monks in the desert, who wore wool and were following the path of poverty. In those days, cotton had just been discovered and was the fashionable thing, whereas wool was the clothing of the poor.

In Islam the way of Christ is associated very much with the way of saintliness: Christ is the prototype of the saint, whereas Muhammad is the prototype of the prophet. Officially, in Islam there is no monasticism, so Sufis are frowned upon because they don't follow the straight and narrow path of Islam. Most of the great Sufis have been executed or exiled for their "free-lance" attitude. So we belong to a line of heretics, and this is a very special honor, because that's true of all the mystics of all religions: they have always been outlawed or just barely within the margins of orthodoxy.

The best protection the Sufis ever had was that people thought they were mad, so they were not taken seriously. And even now, of course, their words make sense only to those who are equally mad; better still, we might say that you have to get yourself into a certain vantage point to make sense of their words. From the ordinary vantage point, they don't make very much sense. It's like having to view a picture from the same point of view as the painter if you want to see it in all its relief. So if a reporter asks you, "What is Sufism?" you have to say, "Well, you have to get into a state of ecstasy in order to be able to see what it is, for I can't explain it in words." As a dervish said to me once, "Never say anything that you think you can say." So we find ourselves in a very difficult position when it comes to a radio show and we try to define what Sufism is in two or three words.

Actually, one of the things very typical of the Sufis is that they claim their inheritance from all the religious traditions, which sounds a note that is very much in tune with our time. That is the aspect of Sufism Hazrat Inayat Khan called "the Message." The Message in our time is the same message as ever before, but the accent is universal. For example, if you were initiated in an ashram in India, you would be given a concentration on the guru of that ashram. But Hazrat Inayat Khan himself gives us concentrations on all the masters, saints, and prophets of all times, which is something that is in the dimension of our time.

Many people would like it if the gurus teaching all the different traditions would at last come together and explain their differences and their similarities and make us feel that we are all together in a great quest. In fact, we have made some attempts to do that, but these attempts are not always successful—or when they are, each one keeps telling his own story, and there is no real interrelationship between them. But we are trying, and I have had seminars with gurus with whom I do feel a very close contact; sometimes we feel we're getting a little bit closer together. Of course we are very close in our feeling, but when it comes to the teachings, it's important to show how it all dovetails—which does not mean that all the teachings are the same. Hazrat Inayat Khan said that unity is not uniformity. So it's far from us to try to create a kind of syncretism.

If we claim the heritage of all the religions of the world, however, we have to know something about them. When we start studying them, we have the impression that there are great contrasts and differences. For example, Buddhism seems atheistic, while Christianity is very God-oriented. There are differences between Islam and Judaism on the one hand and Christianity on the other in that Jews and Muslims do not like the thought that God should become man—it takes away some of the sense of transcendence. Hazrat Inayat Khan's answer to that, of course, is that if you are aware of your inheritance—from your father, for example—you can claim that inheritance; but if you don't know who your father is or cannot claim to have the qualities of your father, then you can't claim your inheritance from him. So if you discover your divine inheritance, you can claim it. That is exactly what Christ says to do: "Be ye perfect as your Father in heaven is perfect" —which is to say that you can also claim your inheritance.

Despite all I've said here, it does look as though the spiritual thinking of humanity is moving forward. You can think of the whole of humanity as being the most potent aspect of the thinking of the planet. You can think of the planet as a being, and you could say that its thinking does proceed. We can't write music as Palestrina did, because the whole thinking nowadays is different. This does not mean that music is better now than it was then, but it is different. There is a process that occurs.

In the early days, at the time when the original teaching of the Hindus and Buddhists came through, people were, of course, aware of the fact of being trapped in the personal vantage point and of a greater consciousness beyond their consciousness, so they stressed the fact that everything is illusion: the way things appear is not the way things are. As the scientists say, "The map is not the territory." It was very obvious to the early Hindus that what we think is the physical universe is not the physical universe, it's just what we think it is; and so they called it *maya* or illusion. This does not mean that physical matter is illusion, but that what we think of it is. The same is true of what we think is our person, and so we should free ourselves from this illusion. The consequence is that one devalues somehow the incarnated condition and seeks a state that is beyond the beyond, in samadhi, for example; and the only way to do this is to make a shift in consciousness from the personal vantage point to the impersonal vantage point—to disidentify oneself with everything that is transient, like the body, mind, personality, and consciousness. These are all called formations, and you get caught in these formations when you identify yourself with them. Because of that, you lose the consciousness of your real being, which is eternal. In other words, you discover your identity in samadhi, and the created condition (which is a Christian term) is devalued. One hopes to free oneself from that condition, at least in one's consciousness, because it's a trap we can get caught up in. This is what the Hindus called "liberation."

The teaching of Hazrat Inayat Khan is really a continuation of the teaching of the Sufis. People sometimes say to someone attending a meditation camp, "Well, you go to that camp, and they are not real Sufis." What are you to answer? You might say, "Well, I thought they were, but maybe you know better." They say, "I am a real Sufi: I have been initiated in the East—the real thing—and this is really phony." This has been said of every Sufi of the past. Al-Hallaj wasn't really in the Sufi tradition, and even Ibn al-'Arabi wasn't. Every Sufi does not repeat what his predecessors said. So Hazrat Inayat Khan does not repeat what al-Hallaj said. People have a tendency to get sclerosed in a certain doctrine, and they can't budge from it. They don't like innovations. It's a very natural thing; there has to be some kind of solidity, otherwise people start floating too much. On the other hand, we can get sclerosed to the extent that there is no progress.

Every teacher, if he really has a contribution to make, is generally in advance of his time. He foresees perspectives that will be taken for granted in fifty years, but in his time they seem a little odd. When we started having the Universal Worship service, in which we light candles for all religions and read the texts of all religions, people were very shocked. That was sixty years ago. Perhaps in some parts of the United States they would still be shocked—and in some parts of Iran, not only would they be shocked, but you might be knifed for putting the Qu'ran on the same altar with the Bible and the "heathen" Buddhist texts. And yet for many people now it is just taken for granted, because the different religions are different aspects of the one religion, which is the religion of God, and the spearhead of civilization has grown into an understanding of the unity behind diversity.

The accent in Hazrat Inayat Khan's teaching is on the importance of being human. The miracle that underscores our lives is that God has become human in us. I could have been burnt as a heretic for saying this not so long ago—and perhaps still could be. Al-Hallaj was crucified for saying something that means the same thing. That God should become human is the whole issue. The orthodox get around it by saying that man manifests some particular qualities of God, but that you can't say that God has become man. They say that man is really like a shadow and that there is no common denominator between God and man; and that is, of course, to maintain the sense of transcendence.

I shall try to be very careful here not to become too philosophical, but one can't help having to express things in terms that involve thinking. At the origin, there is always experience, and then the experience is interpreted by the mind into a kind of system. The mind has a way of generalizing: in my experience, the sun rises every morning, so I assume that it will always rise every morning. The mind tries to account for experience and interprets experience, and that is what is called philosophy: you could say that philosophy is the autopsy of experience. On the other hand, the mind also prefigures experience. For example, according to my experience, the sun turns around the earth—and therefore it took the insight of people who were able to overcome their vantage point to realize that in fact it is the other way around. And still, from my point of view the sun does turn around the earth. In the same way, our thinking can stand in the way of our experience, and we have to change our thinking in order to experience things in the right light. That's the role of metaphysics.

Let us try, then, to translate the word "transcendence" in terms of experience. In meditation, we can see that our bodies are the planet: the substance of the planet has emerged in our bodies just like a wave emerging out of the sea. And we can see that our minds are really the thinking of the planet. Then we would tend to think that what we mean by "God" is the physical universe and the mind of the physical universe, and perhaps the personality behind the universe—all the different levels of reality. By God we mean this One Being—not just one physical body. That is the immanent conception of God: that everything is God.

For a sensitive person, this poses problems, because that would mean that God is also evil—and there is evil, there is no doubt about it. In any case, we can say that nature is fraught with imperfections; if you study science, you will find that there are trials and errors even in biology—in the divine programming. It's not just absolutely perfect. And it's hard to believe that a person who has willfully harmed others is God. So we have the ancient idea that God is up there like a perfect being and what we have down here is only a deviated image of God—God is not all this. That is the extreme sense of transcendence—what Professor Gershom Scholem calls "an exaggerated sense of otherness." But in the human body, for example, we find that there is a great difference between the cells of the hair and nails and the cells of the brain: they all have the same DNA, but the cells of the nails don't have as much latitude or capacity as the cells of the brain. Some cells are produced in a massive way, all alike, and others become more and more specialized, and the specialized cells are extremely complex. In the same way, there are different degrees of godliness in the universe.

A more explicit example would be cancer growth. Cancer is an illness of the DNA: the cancer cell has refused to let itself be coordinated by the DNA of the body and has ordered its DNA so that it does not come under the aegis of the DNA of the body. In other words, it has alienated itself from the order of the universe. So you could say that when beings alienate themselves from the overall order, it is then difficult to say that they are God. Yet they are part of God in the same way that the cancer cell is part of the body and yet not part of the body. Of course, to understand this one must discard syllogistic logic, which attempts to categorize phenomena as one thing or another but does not admit of their being both at the same time. We know now that everything is hybrid: matter is both particle and wave. So we can say that the whole universe is God, and at the same time God is more essentially the DNA of the universe, which is the order behind the universe.

There are some cells that are really key cells, and these cells embody the order much better than others: all cells have the same DNA structure, but somehow that structure is able to come through more perfectly in certain cells. In meditation, you can get into the order behind the universe, which is like getting into the DNA behind the body: you discover the thinking behind the forms. For instance, you can discover the thinking behind a crystal. There is music behind the crystal, of course—a certain resonance—and then frequency; behind that, there is an order, and the matter just lends itself to that order. You can get into a state of randomness if you heat the crystal, and then you get into a different order; but behind everything there is an order.

That order is not static, however. It is a dynamic, inventive order that is continually adapting itself to the feedback it receives in manifestation. So you think of God as dynamic instead of static, and then you realize that that order at times is incredibly complex, like the most challenging toccatas and fugues of Bach. Bach sometimes creates such a very subtle intermeshing of themes that you wonder how on earth he could bring something new out of two totally incompatible themes, and then he moves into altogether new dimensions, then moves on again to something else. In the same way, the order behind the universe, instead of just extending into great complexity and richness, aims at homonization—a word used by Teilhard de Chardin and which means humanization: God becomes human. The DNA of the universe becomes human. The order becomes homonized. The dynamic aspect of God can be seen to move from the rock and the plant to becoming human. And so you realize the importance of the human being, which is exactly what people were trying to get away from in the old traditions—to get away from the human condition into the alpha condition beyond the beyond.

We might say that the early thinking of humanity was cause-oriented while the thinking in our time is purpose-oriented. What is the end purpose of all of this? That God should become human. This is exactly what Hazrat Inayat Khan says all the time: "Divinity is human perfection and humanity is divine limitation." He also says, "The purpose of the whole creation is the realization that God Himself gains by discovering His own perfection through His manifestation." The whole objective is perfection; that is why Christ said, "Be ye perfect as your Father in Heaven is perfect." So there is a complementarity between the teachings of the ancients and the teachings of Hazrat Inayat Khan, which continues the teaching of the Sufis but reaches a great clarity. In fact, it is not just teaching or theory: it's *becoming*. The accent is on becoming rather than on thinking or paying lip service to some belief.

The core of Murshid's teaching was his being. In a big movement that draws a lot of people, there is a force behind it. Jalal ad-din Rumi said, "Everyone was drawn to me to become my friend, but none divined what it was in my heart that drew him." The reason was because he was giving them life, he was giving them ecstasy, and he was giving them insight, among many other things. Behind all that we are doing is the tradition of all the great masters; and as Hazrat

Inayat Khan says, every great master really incorporates all those who came before him. There is a practice among the Sufis of meditating on the masters, and it's a very realistic way of bringing about a change in yourself: getting into the consciousness of a master so that you really experience those qualities as real instead of just trying to imagine divine qualities that are beyond our grasp.

There are very few people living today who have met Hazrat Inayat Khan, and I wish you could have the slightest idea about his being. Wherever he went, he would just fill the whole room with his atmosphere, lift people up by his consciousness, touch people in their soul. His appearance was like that of a king, there was so much majesty and nobility about him, and he had a slow, powerful walk that was nevertheless totally impersonal—it came from a place of deep realization. It's something that happens when one is aware of one's divine inheritance; if you're aware of your personal consciousness, you can't walk that way, you'd be putting it on. But the thing I realize now more and more is the sacredness of Hazrat Inayat Khan's being. These days, it's very rare to come across a person whom you can call a holy man, yet everyone has something sacred in his or her being, and this is what Hazrat Inayat Khan was teaching: to discover and respect the sacredness in every being, the God in you. He was following the precepts of his own teacher, who said, "The only sin is to spend one moment without being in the divine consciousness." And when you follow that practice, the whole being becomes totally sanctified.

Hazrat Inayat Khan was speaking to people, of course, but that was not where things were at, although sometimes he put a whole new insight in a nutshell, which is the strength of his teaching—the ability to say so much in one sentence. But he was and is working on the higher planes, and so very often he would answer a person's question without having to have an interview, and he would look at the person at the time so that that person would know that he knew. Sometimes he would appear in people's dreams and give them answers. So most of the work was done on the higher planes. There is not much use in working with the mind, although there are a lot of psychological groups that have been trying to work with the mind to improve people; some feel they have gained something through it, and some have even been broken. But working with the mind can never give that particular thing that makes a person holy, and, what is more, makes a person awakened.

"Awakening" is a key word: it means we have awakened from our personal vantage point or perspective. Everything looks totally different, and by the fact that you see what lies behind things, you unfold. All the latencies within you manifest. One could say that under the action of the rays of the sun, the buds open up: it just takes that breakthrough of realization to unfold your being. And you could say that your being has been preparing itself for this unfoldment for a long time. There are certain cactuses that build up their sugars for twenty years, and then all of a sudden burst forth in a blaze of colors with a wonderful flower: it's that moment when all the potentialities burst forth into view.

A human being is something like that, although the time element is different. It is possible to go through a long period of incubation when we feel dissatisfied with ourselves because we may be unconsciously aware of a lot of potentialities that are there; then, all of a sudden, the potentialities burst forth. That is what we are aiming at, of course; that's the objective. What it takes to bring about that change is realization: to be freed from a vantage point and awaken from that vantage point so that you suddenly see everything differently—and the practical application of this is that you change.

For example, we assume that we awaken from sleep, but

when you are sleeping you have the impression that you have awakened from your ordinary consciousness, and when you go into deep sleep, you have the feeling that you have awakened from sleep with dreams. So we might say that there are two kinds of awakening, which is exactly what Hazrat Inayat Khan says: God awakening into the physical universe as man; and man, who is God, awakening from his sense of identification with the body into the divine consciousness. Of course, they are both the awakening of God, because in fact there is only one Being.

Here again, we have to overcome our logic, which says that we are only a fraction of the totality. Our logic says, "I am not the physical universe, I am a fraction of the physical universe." In our minds, there is an idea of a frontier: the being has a frontier, and if you identify with your body, that frontier is the skin. To understand that we are both a fraction of the totality and also potentially the totality, we have to overcome our logic. For example, every cell of the body contains the DNA not only of the total body (which means it contains the same structure of molecules), but contains the code of the whole universe. Every fraction contains the totality potentially—it simply isn't active. In the cells of the fingernails, there are only a very few of the aspects of the DNA that are active, whereas in the more advanced cells many more aspects are active; we can use the metaphor of a keyboard with a lot of keys, most of which are Scotch-taped and only some of which are active. So we can say that we are the totality potentially, but in actuation we are a fraction of the totality.

So everything is all one Being, with gradation in it. Essentially—and here is where logic is strained to the utmost—you can think of God as a Being within the more extended being —and perfect within this extended being, which is not perfect. The universe would be the ramifications of this Being. This is very difficult to understand, but the truth is not that simple:

having discovered the order behind the universe, you discover a Being, and it's the being of God. This is not just the total universe, but a very special Being within the more extended being: that little man in the machine that has been so objected to. And you realize this in exactly the same way that a person can awaken into the physical condition or can awaken into a kind of alpha condition beyond the physical condition, into samadhi; but in a human being, one can be awakened only at either one end or the other, while God is awakened at both ends at the same time. So what we mean by awakening is getting into the divine consciousness that is aware of the reality that has become manifest at the physical level *and also* aware of the realization that is gained through the universe.

I said earlier that the order behind the universe, which is like the DNA, is dynamic, not static, and is therefore being continually enriched. Once more defying our logic, God is both dynamic and static. Saint Thomas Aquinas said this, and you'll find the same thing in Meister Eckhart, who makes a contrast between *Gott* and *Gottheit*—He becomes and unbecomes; *Gottheit* is not involved in change or in becoming. When you get into the order of the universe, you realize that it is continually improving itself, so you can't limit God to the order, although it is a very important aspect of the divine Being. You get to a place where there is just intelligence; there is no multiplicity; it's beyond attributes, so it's beyond the order: it's pure intelligence. In fact, that is part of the meaning of the Trinity, which consists of intelligence, pure spirit, and ecstasy.

We should say, then, that God is both static and dynamic, so this Being is both changing and unchanging at some very high level. We could even say that it is an attribute of His perfection to change: it would be limiting if He could not change. So the order takes account of the feedback. Imagine a computer that could program itself by building up information from the environment. You might set it off with a certain program, but in the end it would have a much larger program, because it would have taken into account the feedback from the environment. That would be like the divine order that is continually reprogramming itself and perfecting itself; and yet behind all that there is intelligence.

The original program is like the cause, and that is why many theologians have called God "the Cause," but the programming is not just limited to the cause, because it takes into account the feedback. Everything is not predetermined, because another factor is coming in, and that is the purpose. In biology, for example, the species does not just adapt itself to the environment, it also adapts the environment to its own sense of purpose. So it's an inventive order that is always seeking out new horizons and new possibilities.

There is a feedback, and the information gained is eventually incorporated into the order: what has been gained by God becoming man accrues to the divine consciousness, and that is what we mean by resurrection. So when you say that God awakens beyond manifestation, it does not just mean that He awakens into an alpha state, but that He awakens into a state that includes omega. Samadhi is getting into an alpha state, which is a state of things before the process of becoming —before being involved in the state of becoming; you're suspended beyond time and space. But in the omega state, consciousness is experiencing what has become of alpha by the whole process of life. The emphasis of the teaching of Hazrat Inayat Khan is more on the omega state, which is valuing the importance of life on earth—not limiting reality to the physical body of man or the mind of man or whatever, but including what becomes of man by resurrection. The essence of one's being is extracted from the contingent part. There is a meditation the Sufis perform that is called "working on your body of resurrection"—because, after all, your human condition does not last very long in comparison with the life span of your soul. The accent of Hazrat Inayat Khan's teaching is on discovering the divine purpose becoming a reality in you and working its way towards eternity.

The awakening gives you a very rich way of understanding things, because, as Murshid says, wisdom is a combination of a kind of pre-knowledge that you have with an earthly knowledge that you gain by experience. Most of our thinking is a reaction: we are thinking about things that are related to situations that have occurred in our lives, so our thinking is conditioned. But every now and again there is a thought that is not motivated from outside—a purely spontaneous thought that descends out of "the storehouse of all knowledge" that Hazrat Inayat Khan talks about—and that is a creative thought. In fact, that is what the artist and musician are doing: continually making God a reality in the sense that they are drawing thoughts from the storehouse. When that thought finds its counterpart in a thought that has accrued to you from the outside, then wisdom is complete, as Murshid says. It is like the computer: you have the pre-program and the feedback, and the feedback would be like the thought that has accrued to you from the outside.

For example, if you say a table is round, it's because roundness is part of a kind of pre-thought—an archetypal thought in your soul—and when you recognize that roundness in an object, you say that the table is round. Or if you see a sunrise and it makes you feel very elated, it is because somehow you have the memory of being a being of light, and the sunrise just reminds you of what you are. So wisdom is complete when there is a perfect matching between your intuitive knowledge and your practical knowledge. That is what is gained by life, because the pre-knowledge remains incomplete until it has been substantiated by the feedback.

Another aspect of what Hazrat Inayat Khan teaches is that

we digest experience. For example, there is a difference between the taste of food in your mouth and the taste of food in your stomach. Most people don't know the taste in their stomach, or the taste in their pancreas, but if you feel sick you certainly do. That is a deeper kind of assimilation of knowledge. In the same way, there is a knowledge of the mind that gets filtered down deeper into your soul when it is assimilated. When it is assimilated in your being, you have to change a lot of things in your being in order to be able to incorporate this knowledge, and so it becomes a transforming knowledge. In consequence, one becomes very, very deep.

Hazrat Inayat Khan says that if you identify yourself with being a body, then you will be aware of the bodies of people or of objects; if you identify yourself with your mind, you will be aware of the thoughts of people, conversing at the thought level; if you are aware of your heart, then you will be picking up the emotions of people; but if you are aware of your soul, you will be communicating at the soul level. And he makes a distinction between the emotion of the soul and the emotion of the heart: the emotion of the heart can be rather sentimental and even rather mushy, but the emotion of the soul is very, very deep; when you have touched upon that emotion, you realize how much deeper and more meaningful it is for you. The whole teaching of Murshid comes from that very deep place—from the soul rather than the heart or the mind. And behind the teaching—behind words and thinking—there is emotion, and it is the emotion of the universe.

You may watch a wonderful sunrise, or enjoy a storm or a rainbow or walking in the mountains, or listening to wonderful music or to the babbling of children, or talking with wonderful people, or being in love, or just the emotions you are exposed to. You may even get into the consciousness of your dog or a butterfly or a tree or a crystal, and in so doing get into the thinking of the butterfly or the thinking of the crystal or of the tree—or even the emotion of the butterfly or the tree. But there is a still deeper place that you can get into, and that is the emotion that became the tree, or the thinking that became the tree: not the thinking *of* the tree, but the thinking that *became* the tree. Instead of experiencing the emotion of the stars and the planets, you experience the emotion that has manifested as the emotion of the planets. It's much deeper—a totally different dimension of emotion—and that's the emotion Murshid was conveying, because that was the emotion that he was experiencing. People might not have known it, but he was transporting them into that emotion.

So not only are our bodies part of all the totality, and not only are our minds part of all this, but we are also invited to enter into the thinking behind all of this. What is more, we *are* part of the thinking behind all of this. That is awakening, and, better still, realization. You awaken from your vantage point and have access into the mind of God—which leads toward the discovery that you *are* the being of God. The consequence is that you become totally transformed, transfigured: the Sufis call it *akhlak-e Allah,* which means that you begin to adopt the manner of God. Wherever you go, you bring this attunement, this consciousness, this realization with you. That is the ultimate objective of the spiritual life. We are invited to do this, and it may be the state of consciousness of people in the future. We are just on our way towards that; and once you have tasted of it, you realize that that is what it's all about. It is the objective for which we were born.

# CHAPTER 14

# "O Man, If You Only Knew that You Are Free"

We must have our objective very clearly in view, even though it's like the horizon: as you advance it recedes, and therefore you can never really grasp it—which is very good. Otherwise you would reach a point where there is nothing more to do, or to attain, or to achieve. Defining objectives is, of course, limitation, but we have to do it. It gives us at least a direction if not a clear objective—an azimuth, or several azimuths.

The first objective we seek is freedom. We often have a very pragmatic understanding of freedom; we think that being free means to be free to express opinion, and so forth. Whenever we see that political freedom has been curbed, we rise against this, because we feel that something very sacred has been alienated from the human being. In fact, the great issue in politics at all times—and particularly in our time—is freedom. But in the spiritual realm, when we speak about freedom we mean freedom from the ego, and that requires explanation, of course.

The second objective is achievement. Not just achieving things, but achieving things in a meaningful way. That cuts right into a grave problem, which is understanding and fulfilling the purpose of our lives. If you had the opportunity to sit in the presence of someone with great insight into your being, the first thing you would ask is, "How can I achieve the purpose of my life?" The word "purpose" may be a little vague, and you might not quite know what it means, but it does involve your job, it might involve your personal relationships, and it might involve your dedication to the spiritual life—and then we have to define exactly what that means.

Achievement involves, essentially, mastery. As Hazrat Inayat Khan said, "When a rider has no strength in his fingers, he cannot hold the horse's reins. His fingers must obey his mind before the horse will obey. This is true of all circumstances in life." In other words, if you have mastery over yourself, you will have mastery over circumstances; if things go wrong, it means that you do not have mastery over yourself, so you can find the source in yourself.

These questions are all interrelated, of course, because if you're free inside, it makes it much easier for you to achieve your purpose, while on the other hand, our achievement is very much connected with the unfoldment of our being. When we have a sense of purpose in our lives, we unfold the qualities that are needed in our lives to meet that purpose.

This is the next purpose—the unfoldment of our being. We are the Pygmalion of our personality, as Murshid says. The divine art, which is all creation, is continued in the human being, and carried further in the art of personality. It is carried further in all forms of art, of course, but mainly in the highest and ultimate art, which is the art of personality. So one of our objectives is building a beautiful world of beautiful people.

The next purpose is realization, which is also called awakening—awakening from the point of view in which we are sclerosed, and seeing things in a different perspective. These three objectives—achievement, unfoldment, and realization —are all very closely connected, because it is your self-discovery and your realization of your inheritance—you could call it your potentiality if you like—that enable your qualities to become manifested, or to become real.

There are more purposes, which are, of course, also all connected. One of these is being in a state of ecstasy—being in a very high state of attunement. You become very sensitive to the emotions of people when you walk in the streets of the planet. Sometimes you realize how bored people seem to be, how low-key, whereas once you have discovered the emotion behind the universe, you are attuned to a very high key, and the consequence is that you carry everyone in your ecstasy. This is part of building a beautiful world.

The next objective is illumination, which can be found in those moments when you feel you're aware of being a being of light. You realize that your body is the physical incorporation of a body that was pure light, and with this realization comes a memory of the heavenly spheres. Then your whole being is transformed and becomes absolutely radiant. Your eyes begin to glow. This can be carried even further: you can work upon your insight as being luminous, like a light that is cast upon all things to make them clear. Or you might experience illumination when you're sitting talking to a person and the whole environment seems to be transfigured—there's a lot of light shining in the eyes of the person with whom you're speaking, and you know that you yourself are beginning to glow—you're experiencing a communion of light. You get to a point where wherever you go, you're aware of casting your light upon all things.

Of course, there are more objectives, such as being so full of life energy that you give energy to everybody. There are some people who, wherever they go, make a success of the situations in which they find themselves, because they have this wonderful influence—a kind of dynamizing influence. They're putting energy into all things. A good example of this is Prince Puran, who was banished by his father, became a sannyasin, and then returned to the garden of the palace. Since he had left the palace, the garden had become a desert, but as soon as he sat there, everything began to flourish. There are schools that work very largely with energy, but there is a danger in simply working with energy without always casting the light of consciousness upon the way the energy is used. In nature, we find that most phenomena are the result of energy: energy is expended in bringing about phenomena, and this is accompanied by an increase of information and therefore an increase of consciousness, so consciousness is always increasing at the cost of energy. As energy runs down, there's a loss of order, which is the real meaning of entropy.

The best example of entropy is a library. If all the books are out of place, there's a leveling out—the energy of the library has been lost. The energy is in the order of it; in fact, it takes energy to put the books back into place again. The world is running down in the sense that the whole universe is moving from an original state of order to leveling out, while on the other hand there's a building up of order at another level, which is the level of realization. There's been an increase in disorder, and there's been an increase in order. In our civilization, for example, an enormous amount of order goes into the simplest things, like security and precautions and regulations. Everything is much more ordered in society now than it was forty or fifty years ago. But on the other hand, there's never been so much chaos.

If you look at nature, you see the same thing. Most of the

phenomena that are observed by the physicists are phenomena
of disintegration of matter—like radiation, which is disintegration of matter. In biology, the phenomena that are
observed are the building up of organisms out of the
breakdown of matter. And on the psychological level, there's a
still greater build-up at the cost of the living substance.

So on the one hand there is disorder, which really means
randomness. There was a time when it was thought that
nothing happened without the wish of God, and it is a very
great question whether there is such a thing as randomness.
The fact is, randomness applies to disintegration. In the
building up there's free will. We might say that the purpose of
the human being is not just to manifest the divine potentialities, but even to manifest the divine will freely. There is a
tradition in the Qu'ran that God spoke to the souls of men
when they were still in the loins of Adam—that is, when they
were pure latencies—and asked them, "Will you declare my
sovereignty?" And they answered, "I will!" It was that "I
will" that established their relative autonomy. That's where
free will comes in.

The same thing happens in our meditations: there are
meditations that are random, and there are meditations that
are very highly ordered. A lot of people say, "Well, when I
meditate, I don't like to have too many themes. I just let
myself go and experience myself as a part of all things and I
have a wonderful feeling of being high." That's randomness.
It's nice, but it's not really creative. For it to be creative, you
have to become aware of the divine order behind the universe.
The same is true in art: Johann Sebastian Bach is expressing
the divine order in music. The awareness of the divine order is
the saving grace that overcomes the terrible despair we
sometimes feel when we see the disorder in the minds of
people.

The last objective is sacredness. That's a very difficult thing to put one's finger on, but it's something that happens to a person by the consciousness of the divine presence, or the consciousness of being the custodian of the Holy Grail and having therefore to protect the sacredness that is the essence of all beings. So there is a great respect for all beings, even if they act in a disgraceful way, because you are aware of the divine Presence suffering in limitation and yet always perfect.

Now we want to see how we can make these objectives as concrete as possible in our lives—how we can work with ourselves, in our thoughts and our emotions, to bring about a change. It would be a good idea if, every day, in addition to any other practices you do, you would give yourself time to look upon your life in the light of these objectives and see very concretely how you can apply these objectives in real situations.

The first thing to do is to be quite sure that you don't just take for granted that the physical world is as it appears. There's a tendency to get bogged down in, and even rather depressed by, the kind of artificiality that people have made of nature. The only way of freeing yourself from the terrible pressure of the appearance of physical reality is by switching your consciousness off from its ordinary focus so that you get into a transfigured state. You can do this simply by offsetting your glance and not allowing it to be bullied into normal focus. If you keep on doing it, you'll begin to develop the glance of the ascetic. It's part of a whole inner attunement— it's not letting yourself be fooled. You don't let yourself be caught up in the ordinary framework of time and space. Once you experience yourself as eternal, then you get into the transfigured state. Time stands still: you're meeting people beyond time and space. It's being high without drugs. And the way to do it is not to forget what you really are. You're aware that you're experiencing things on the planet, but you're like the visitor from outer space, so you don't let yourself get jammed into the circumstances in which you find yourself.

It is also very helpful to remember what Shihab ad-din Suhrawardhi said about that which transpires behind that which appears. What you experience normally, what hits your retina, is that which appears; but beyond that is that which transpires. That's a rather vague phrase—"that which transpires." It might mean several things—and, in fact, it does mean several things. For example, if you had eyes to see, you would see the auras of the trees and of people, and you'd see the eternal faces of people behind their features. Sometimes an apparently plain person may have an extremely beautiful eternal face, and a person who would pass in the world for being beautiful may not have so beautiful an eternal face. The appearance isn't always something to go by, because the substance of the face is made out of the fabric of the planet, with all its deficiencies—just as there might be a statue made of a very inadequate substance that would still be beautiful because of what came through. This would be a very concrete example of that which transpires behind that which appears.

There are other ways of understanding that which transpires behind that which appears. When you're looking at a flower, there is a kind of life force that comes through—that transpires. As in the case of Prince Puran, you come to a point where you are conscious of continually giving out life—*prana,* or magnetism—and then you feel that in other beings. In fact, when you start feeling it in other beings, you start drawing it into yourself and charging yourself with energy. The more energy you give out, the more energy you receive.

Another thing that transpires is emotion. You get to the point where you become very sensitive to emotion; you might even become very touchy about vulgar emotions. It's a sign of spiritual unfoldment. In fact, you might almost say that every person is in his place in life according to the quality of his emotion. And, of course, thought transpires. Then there is something further that transpires, which is the cause behind the cause and the purpose beyond the purpose.

What we want to know now, though, is how to apply the principle of liberation. How do we apply our nostalgia for liberation in the nitty-gritty of everyday life? We started by freeing ourselves from the appearance of the physical world. Now we have to talk about our self-image. It is easy to become stuck in our self-image; we pride ourselves on what we like to think we are while at the same time we suffer from fear of inadequacy and even from self-degradation.

Because of this, you can suffer greatly in the most vulnerable aspect of your being, which is your sense of self-esteem. You are obviously caught in a perspective; it is an illusion, and in fact you are not what you think you are. It is a wonderful freedom to realize this; it's such a wonderful experience to be without a mask. It's to be "the nameless and the formless," to "walk without feet and fly without wings," as Shems-i Tabriz said. This is also something you can practice in everyday life—being free from your personality.

This may seem strange, because we did say that we are the artists of our personality. But in order to change our personality, we have to let go of it first. It has to be disintegrated before it's rebuilt. We can't just work with our personality as one would work with an object like a piece of ceramics. You have to go through a breakdown before you can experience a breakthrough. That's the whole meaning of the alchemical process.

People often come up to me and say, "Pir, can you help me to become a better person? All you have to do is to tell me what my defects are, and I'll try to work on them." Never let yourself into that hornets' nest; as soon as you say, "Yes, well, you have these qualities, and then you have these defects," the person is on his high horse, defending himself, because nobody likes to be criticized. And quite rightly, because people are so vulnerable in their sense of self-esteem. But if you're so touchy about yourself and your sense of self-esteem, how can you improve yourself? You may even be justifying unconsciously your defects to yourself, while at the same time criticizing yourself, while you still don't like other people to criticize you. A human being is a very complex and rather irrational being.

We are continually suspended on the horns of a dilemma, between freedom and fulfillment; or, if you like, between renunciation or detachment on the one hand and enthusiasm on the other. There are moments when you have to apply detachment and freedom to your self-image, and there are times when you have to apply enthusiasm. The beauty of being totally impersonal is not being stuck anymore in your personality, and therefore your personality is able to disintegrate. That's freedom: you renounce your personality. It's much more useful than renouncing your home to go and live in the forest: it's a much subtler thing.

The counterpart of this is that you experience the miracle of being the fashioner of your personality. You have to first disintegrate it before you reintegrate it, and that's where freedom comes in.

Hazrat Inayat Khan talks about testing yourself at every moment in your life to see how free you are. When you're being criticized, and particularly insulted, but even just criticized, that's when you're tested in your freedom. It's a great thing if you can reach a point where it doesn't affect you emotionally, and perhaps the only thing you can say in your defense is, "It's all a matter of opinion." If you start defending yourself, you're entering into a battle of wits, and your adversary might be cleverer than you, so that you begin to feel very dejected. You must feel that it doesn't matter—that if your personality impresses people or doesn't impress people, it doesn't matter. Who cares? That's what it means to be free.

Now we come to a very essential thing that you must think about every day, and that is your involvement with people and situations and your freedom. But you must also remember that our objective is not just freedom, it is fulfillment, so we should really consider these two objectives at the same time. If you were an ascetic, then you would just consider freedom. You would try to observe and scrutinize your life and find out what were the circumstances in which you allowed your freedom to be alienated.

The best example of this is an ascetic that I knew, a wonderful man. He was a sannyasin and had lived in the forest in India for ten years, and he would just sit for hours meditating. He was so peaceful that all kinds of animals would pass by and never attack him. Sannyasins seek a cave and then make a vow that they will stay there for a certain number of years and do their practices. He had found a cave that was near water, and no one was there; so he thought, "This is just wonderful." So he went to bathe in the river, and all of a sudden an enormous tiger came and started bounding toward him at high speed. He started sweating and trembling, but then he thought, "After all, I'm supposed to master myself." He told me that he really was afraid, but he didn't want to run away because he was supposed to master himself. And he said he couldn't believe it, but at the last minute the tiger stopped and started licking his feet and purring. So all his sweat dried up, and although he didn't quite, that first time, dare to pet the tiger, he had overcome his fear. And then when he used to go and bathe in the river, the tiger would come and bathe with him.

The same man told me that once he was in the forest, just meditating, and when he rose out of his meditation he found that the beggar's bowl he had for his water was missing. He wondered what on earth could have happened to it. He thought that perhaps he might have forgotten it at the place where he was bathing, so he went and looked along the river. It wasn't there. "Could I have left it in my cave?" No; not there. So he kept on searching the jungle for his beggar's bowl, until he suddenly said to himself, "Just imagine—I spent all of this time out of my anxiety for my property." He would tell this story when he was out in the world and talking to people, and he would say, "You with all your possessions, how do you expect to be able to meditate, if I spent so much time worrying about my one possession?"

So the way of the ascetic is to give everything up, because he feels that that is the only way to be totally free. What Hazrat Inayat Khan is trying to teach us is much more difficult: to be free while involving ourselves with people and with circumstances, because we're both the ascetic and the knight, not just the ascetic. That's much more difficult. For example, can you consider your material goods to be an instrument of action? Then it's all right to have them. But I remember a friend of mine who had a magnificent house in Los Angeles. He was retired, and it was a very famous house, so people used to come to visit the house, and he was just the caretaker of it. If he had been imbued with the spirit of the ascetic, then instead of building a beautiful house he would have become a beautiful person by giving up the house. He could have given up the house for refugees or for education or rehabilitation or for some other purpose.

I'm not saying that you should give up your house or your car. You simply consider them as instruments of action. But you have to be internally free, so that if all of a sudden everything should be taken away from you, it wouldn't affect you at all. That would be freedom—freedom from crass material paraphenalia. That is why a millionaire, if he goes bankrupt, will often commit suicide, whereas the dervish, if he has any money, will give it away. The dervish doesn't care for money at all.

There are many other things, of course, that can affect you—for example, your position in your job. Looking around, I have the impression that most people are really underemployed. That means that people have many more gifts than they can ever use. That's the way things are for the moment. I like to think that it's just the way society is planned, with the accent on material well-being at the cost of human creativity. People are beginning to become aware of that, and are not wanting to be just part of a system; they want to be able to fulfill themselves in their jobs instead of just fitting into a big machine. People feel degraded in their ability by being underemployed.

Of course, you can do everything possible to place yourself in a situation that is conducive to the unfoldment of your being, but if you cannot, your only protection will be freedom from the outer position. In reality, no one can take away from you what you are, and nobody can give you what you're not. Your real status has nothing to do with the outer appearance. There might be a king on a throne who's a fool, and a street-sweeper who's a genius. I knew a waitress at a coffee shop in the Chicago airport, and I don't know whether she knows how much I've talked about her. She just kept the whole coffee shop in hysterics of laughter, and everything she said was so wise. She was a real guru acting under the guise of a waitress. After seeing her, I realized that whatever the outer position is, it's not important. What you do with it is what's important. If you're really up tight about the outer thing, then of course you're going to suffer, so perhaps the best thing to do is to apply the principle of holding your head high and being conscious of the divine perfection in the middle of limiting circumstances.

Hazrat Inayat Khan said the dervish is the real king. The

word "king," of course, embodies the sense of pride that people have—and suffer from, and judge themselves by, and are criticized for, and so on. But Murshid really makes it clear when he says spirituality is "the aristocracy of the soul and the democracy of the ego."

So in every human being there is a dichotomy between the sense of pride and the sense of inadequacy. But if it's rightly placed, your pride is in your divine inheritance—in your consciousness of the divine perfection. And your inadequacy is in being aware of the limitation you impose upon the divine perfection in yourself. It is particularly important for an idealist to realize that the circumstances will never be ideal. What you can do is handle circumstances in an ideal way. That's what most of us are fretting about all the time: "If only .... Why can't it be...?" That's the limitation in which the divine perfection is functioning. Think of Christ functioning in that limitation: think of what those Roman soldiers did! Of course, it wasn't just the soldiers; they were under instructions. But think what they did to this being—what a terrible crime it was to treat such perfection in that way.

Sometimes the circumstances in which you are functioning are just absolutely frustrating. Wherever you turn, you're blocked. That is the moment to be conscious that the divine perfection itself is continually suffering from the limitation of circumstances. There's no use fighting. You fight as much as you can, but the only way to deal with the problem is to find perfection by integrating another plane. It's like three-dimensional chess: if you find that you're jammed on one plane, you can always resort to the next one. For example, a woman might be married to someone who is a bully, who comes home grouchy and pushes her to the corner—it's as if she had no space to be: he just fills the house with his ego. It may be the other way around, of course—it may be the wife who is the bully. But in both circumstances, generally one person has a very strong ego and always wins, and the other is often a very fine person who can't use the kind of weapons that are used by the ego. So this is a very clear case where the sense of freedom comes into play: if you're the martyred one, your only defense is absolute freedom from your ego, because your ego doesn't get any satisfaction in that situation, that's for sure. But on the other hand, you have to be able to find a higher space where the person with the strong ego is unable to reach you. Then that person gets terribly frustrated, because you have something that he can't reach; he'll try to pull you down into his realm. What he wants is for you to fight him, because he knows he will always win. If you run into that trap, of course you never get out of it; and if you don't fight, then he gets angry that you don't fight and tries to entice you into fighting by getting angry. Your detachment is your defense: no one can get you there.

It's only freedom that will give you the power to meet that kind of situation. It's freedom from your self-esteem, because what that person will do is criticize you all the time—attack you in your self-esteem, because that's the way to undermine a person. If you try to keep on defending yourself—and you probably don't have the kind of ego that is able to defend itself —the consequence is that he can really make you plunge into the depths of despair, unless you are totally detached from your sense of personal pride in your ego. You can only have pride in your eternal, divine inheritance. If he attacks your ego, it's just like hitting the air, because there's nothing there. He can't touch you. Keeping your pride in the divine consciousness is very powerful.

Our involvement with people is extremely important. This is something one should think about every day, as part of the transition between meditation and everyday life. Have you allowed yourself to be talked into something or to be bullied into a situation by the ego of another person? If you have, the consequence is suffering, because you have alienated your freedom. That's the reason why the ascetic eventually finds himself in the woods—because he will not compromise in any way. In dealing with the circumstances in life, it's very difficult not to compromise.

I knew of a man whose father was a very rich wine merchant, and one day the son found out that his father was selling inferior wine as good quality wine because it had a good name. So he told his father, "I can't go along with this." He had signed a contract with his father, and he was bound by that contract; in other words, he was bound to do something against his conscience. He was jammed because he was bound by his contract with his father—and the result was that his father disowned him. He knew he was running the risk of that, but he went ahead and spoke to his father anyway, and consequently he was free inside. If he had kowtowed to the situation because he knew that he would lose his fortune by standing up for what he believed to be true, he would have lost his freedom.

This is an extreme example, but it's typical of what can happen in life. In the words of Christ, "What is a man profited, if he shall gain the whole world, and lose his own soul?" You only have yourself to live with, and if you are living in wealth and find that you have a bad conscience, you can't possibly be happy.

So you can apply the way of the ascetic in life by always watching your freedom. Of course, there is a question of the personal involvement you have with the person you love—your husband, wife, girlfriend, boyfriend, or whoever. It's obviously an involvement, which means, of course, an alienation of freedom to some extent—an alienation of the freedom of the individual. What is gained is a kind of joint freedom. Two notes of a piano together form a chord, and the chord is more than the two notes, it's a new reality; in the same way, a relationship is a new reality that arises at the cost of the freedom of each individual to some extent.

Eagles are always in couples, and it's amazing to see how their pride is such that neither of them wants to follow the other, as some of the smaller birds do. You'll find one of them flying in one direction and the other going in just the opposite direction—and they're always watching each other. If one of them really goes too far, then the other one gets into a panic and does follow, but then he sees that the other one was trying him out as far as possible and probably wouldn't have gone much farther if he hadn't panicked. There's just this testing on both sides.

This is also typical of human relationships, not only in the love relationship but also in friendship. People try each other as far as they can—it's a battle of wills. In fact, it's amazing that two people ever get to be able to coordinate their lives, because people have different wills. It's particularly bad if it's always the same person who gives in. It's very bad both for the person who gives in and for the person to whom the other gives in; and once you start, then it gets worse and worse. That's where your freedom will help keep you from stumbling into a position of dependence. Even in a love relationship, people have egos. The ego of a person is supposed to be overcome by the power of love, but that would be an idyllic situation. In practice, it's very rare that the love of a person is so great that he or she can overcome the ego totally, so love can subject you to another person's ego, and your only protection is to maintain somewhat the spirit of the sannyasin. You'll find in the end that the person who's been trying it on you will respect you more and love you more than if you'd given in. So this is a very clear case of applying the way of the sannyasin directly in a situation that is the opposite of the way of the sannyasin, which is the life of relationship.

Many people find themselves in a situation where the

person they thought loved them ceases to love them. I've known cases in which people got into such a deep depression that they even went into a state of schizophrenia. Here again, it is only the attitude of detachment that will help you to be able to stand the strain. In fact, this can be applied even in the course of the love relationship between two people: you can love a person without depending on being loved. In that case, you are applying the principle of the sannyasin to life in relationship. When it's the other way around—if you depend upon being loved—then you will be disappointed.

In fact, if people feel that you depend upon their love, sometimes they will turn away; but if they know that you are free, they will be drawn to you. The reason for this is that if you are free, you're freeing them. Essentially, in every being there is a need for freedom. No one likes to feel dependent upon another—or perhaps we should say that people sometimes like to feel dependent upon another, but when they have to incur the ultimate consequence of that dependence they don't like it.

So these are several ways of applying the way of the sannyasin to the way of the world. In order to be able to see the situation very clearly, you have to look upon yourself as the visitor from outer space who has landed on the planet and drawn towards himself a body made of the fabric of the planet in order to experience conditions on the planet, and who then got involved with people and circumstances here. From that point of view, you can see your involvement very clearly— where you are involved, what it means, and what the outcome of it is; and, of course, the outcome is of enormous value. You mustn't see it negatively, because involvement is extremely important. The outcome of it is that out of the osmosis between beings—out of the cross-pollination of beings—each being is enriched. There's more in your personality than the seed of your personality, because your personality is enriched by your connection with other beings; in fact, everything is enriching your personality.

Dive deeply into the miracle of life and let the tips of your wings be burnt by the flame, let your feet be lacerated by the thorns, let your heart be stirred by human emotion, and let your soul be lifted beyond the earth. Let your life be a full involvement without being a trap, always maintaining the consciousness of the divine perfection in you and maintaining your freedom of thought. Do you realize how you can be caught in a certain way of thinking and not see that it's just a perspective? The proof of it is that maybe some time ago you wanted something, and now you're sorry that it ever happened —or you're glad that it didn't happen. At that time, you saw things in a certain way; now you're free.

Many people get caught in cults. You might ask them, "Why do you believe this?" "Oh, well, I've always believed it." "But *why* do you believe it?" "Yes, that's a good question. Well, yes, I've been brought up to believe it." "Yes, but I mean why? Because people told you it was so?" "Yes, yes. People told me." "Well, why do you believe it because people told you? Maybe their opinion could be wrong." "Yes, I suppose. I never thought that their opinion could be wrong." "Well, do you *have* to believe this?" "No, perhaps I don't have to believe it." "Well, then, you're free—you don't have to believe it, do you?" "Yes, I'm free!" That's freedom. All this time you'd thought this, and all of a sudden you think, "Well, I don't have to think that. Why do I have to think that? It was just a habit. I'm free."

So you see how a group of people can catch you in a certain perspective, and that's where you need deprogramming. Our whole life is like that. Farid ad-din Attar said, "O man, if you only knew that you are free"; it is your thinking that you are not free that is your prison. You might say, "But there are the circumstances; I can't change those circumstances, and I'm caught in those circumstances." But you can be free inside and bound by circumstances—just as you could be bound inside and free in circumstances. Do you think that if you left your job and went wandering to India—as many people do— that you would then be free? That only makes the outer circumstances free; it doesn't make *you* free.

The real freedom manifests internally: the outer circumstances do not affect you. The real freedom lies in never letting yourself get caught up in a certain way of thinking; you never get yourself caught in opinion, including your own opinion. It's a wonderful protection. If a person starts arguing, you could get hot under the collar and argue against him—but it would be wasting so much time. All you have to say is, "I don't value opinion, and that includes my own opinion." It's a perspective; we tend to get caught in a perspective. As al-Hallaj says, if only you had access to the divine understanding, your own understanding would be shattered. So much time is wasted getting caught in opinions and perspectives. Free yourself from them. It's better to spend time meditating—at least then you're in a totally different realm of experience.

There are several other forms of freedom. For example, freedom from fear, which is what the sannyasin facing the tiger gained. There's a little test you can take: ask yourself, "Now, if I were asked to throw myself down with a parachute from a plane, would I do it?" "Oh, no, I couldn't do it." But of course you can do it. People do it; why can't you? Overcome fear. Facing a person who has a terrible ego may make you tremble; you may not know how to face that person. But there again, you can overcome fear. You can own up to things, even if you're afraid that it will be a terrible hassle or that there might be a terrible row, so that you would rather just not own up and not talk about it. Come forth; you become much stronger. You can become free from fear.

There are practical ways of applying our meditations to our daily problems—tangible ways to achieve our spiritual objectives in life.

# CHAPTER 15

# The Purpose of Life

[A Meditation at the Dargah of Hazrat Inayat Khan]

We are here in New Delhi at the tomb of my father, Hazrat Inayat Khan, to commemorate the departure of his soul, and perhaps it's a moment when we should just evoke his memory. You have probably been moved, as I have been, by the experience of coming to Delhi and seeing all these children rushing up to you. It reminds me very much of Hazrat Pir-o-Murshid Inayat Khan, because there were swarms of children wherever he was, and I was among them. Now it's the reverse, of course.

I saw Hazrat Inayat Khan from the point of view of a child. In Sufism, one learns how to see another through his eyes, so maybe I was looking at Murshid through his eyes and he was looking at me through my eyes. Or maybe Murshid was seeing himself through the eyes of a child. I remember seeing him walking down the steps of Fazal Manzil, our home in Suresnes, near Paris. We children used to lie in the grass and wait for the moment when he was going to come down the steps. We didn't have a watch, but we had a kind of intuition that the time was drawing near, so we dropped all our toys or whatever we were playing with, because this was the most important thing in our lives. Then the door opened and we could see him emerging and walking down the steps like a king. In fact, the first thing that impressed us most was the majesty of his being: he walked down with very slow, majestic steps, like a powerful elephant.

Then we didn't see him for some time, because he was crossing the road; and then he would come and walk across the field where we were lying. As he walked, he seemed to be carrying the whole world on his back, and we lay absolutely spellbound by all that was coming through him. Now, of course, we were discovering other aspects we hadn't seen before. We were discovering power—a power that was so great that it seemed it could remove mountains. And yet it was a power that one could never be afraid of. Power can be very frightening, but here was a power that was full of kindness. Of course, we as children learned to respect his being because of what he was, so that at no time did he ever have to affirm his power. But it was there, and when we were children that was what disciplined us. Children tend to feel how nice it is to do all the things that are naughty, and will always see how much they can outsmart their parents. We were naughty children, too. But Murshid never so much as had to raise his voice: perhaps he would raise an eyebrow, and we would know that we couldn't outsmart him.

There were always guests at meals, so Hazrat Inayat Khan always had a little table for the children so they could chat without having to feel frustrated by the adults, because normally if we were sitting at the big table the only thing we were ever allowed to say was, "Please pass me the salt." At times, Murshid would suddenly reveal himself to be the most wonderful father, full of love for his children. He always found time to tell us a good-night story before we went to bed. When I think of it now, I realize that it meant he might have had to drop a lot of interviews and committee meetings and all kinds of things for that simple moment when we were able to sit on his lap and he told us all those stories that you read in Idries Shah's books nowadays. Sometimes, like all children, we were interested in the story, but I think that what was most meaningful to us was the way he told it to us. We would ask him again and again to explain to us why the story happened the way it did and what it would have been like if it were different.

There was a lady whose unfortunate job it was always to tell us to be quiet. Of course, we always thought of her as being a very hard disciplinarian, but actually she was the most wonderful *mureed* of Hazrat Inayat Khan. She was Murshida Sherifa Goodenough; and if there was anyone who knew absolutely his thought and emotion and everything about Murshid, it was Murshida Sherifa Goodenough. Whenever Murshid went anywhere, except when he was walking up to the hall, when he was alone because he had to keep his magnetism, he was always surrounded by three ladies: Murshida Sherifa Goodenough, Nekbakht Furnée, and Kismet Stam. All three of them used to take notes of the lectures to ensure getting an accurate record of what Murshid said. Murshida Sherifa Goodenough sometimes seemed rather curt with us, always saying there was no time and we had to behave ourselves and all that sort of thing. But Murshid would always tell us why.

Especially in those days, people used to tell a child to do this and do that. Murshid always used to say why. And of all people, of course, he was the most busy, but he took time to tell us why. You know how important that question is; in fact, Murshid calls it "the big mountain, 'Why?'" He took the trouble to tell us. Even when there was a hurry he would say why, although once he said, "I have to be brief because there's not much time." And I remember him once saying, "Well, Vilayat, you couldn't understand. But as soon as you are old enough to understand, then I'll tell you why." That was wonderful, because I was used to him always telling me why, and I knew that the only reason he couldn't say it this time was because I wasn't old enough to understand.

This gave us a confidence in Murshid that he would never tell anyone to follow him blindly. That's a policy I've followed all my life: never to tell people what to do. You can absolutely ruin people's lives by telling them, "You should do this," or, "You should do that." This is not only because you might not understand all the different aspects of a problem—in the case of Murshid, how could that have been? It is because by telling people what to do you are taking away their sense of responsibility and making them into puppets. So here was the very incorporation of wisdom, who could always see exactly what the issue of the problem was, and who nevertheless, out of respect for you, always refrained from telling you what to do.

When we read the teachings of Hazrat Inayat Khan, we understand how he saw into problems. I thought I used to know his teachings, but the fact is one can never know the extent of them. He was seeing the cause behind the cause and the purpose beyond the purpose. Most people see the effect; he was always seeing behind it, seeing the cause. And, of course, he was showing us how to develop intuition. If you go into his teaching, you'll see that intuition means that you really have to get into the consciousness of another person, which is one of the things I'm teaching all the time—getting into the consciousness of a person—and, what is more, experiencing the condition of the person in yourself. For example, when you come across a person who is brutal, all the brutality in you comes up, doesn't it? And even if you don't have any ego, when you're facing a person with a strong ego, it makes you feel like fighting him. If you're faced with a person who is dishonest, then any kind of dishonesty in you—and there is dishonesty in everyone—comes up. Every time you say, "Hello, it's so nice to see you," when you don't mean it, there's dishonesty; every time you think you have to be tactful about a situation, there's dishonesty. There is some dishonesty in everyone, and when you are faced with a dishonest person, it comes up.

So here was another aspect of Murshid that I began to discover as I grew up. Murshid is so multi-dimensional: in the course of my youth and adulthood, I passed through different ways of looking upon him. As a very small child, I discovered the aspect of majesty, which impressed me so much then; and later on, power. Then it was wisdom. As I grew a little older and started to go to the university, I was faced with the wisdom of the world. I always felt there was something wrong about the wisdom of the world, but as you know, when one is very young one doesn't really see what is wrong with it; it just doesn't feel right. And I had the terrible problem of reconciling what I was learning at the university, which was philosophy, with what Hazrat Inayat Khan was saying. They didn't seem compatible in the least. Now, of course, looking back upon it all, it's become very clear how our thinking is based upon logic, and as soon as you see how fallacious logic is, then you're not fooled by it any longer. Most people are fooled by it. Later on, when I went to Oxford, there was a saying about philosophy that the philosopher is "a blind man who is searching in a dark room for a black cat that isn't there." At that time, I suppose I was that blind man—and I couldn't find the black cat either. But somehow I remember that Murshid knew all the time that there wasn't a black cat there, because he was endowed with a greater wisdom—the wisdom that sees into the soul.

Hazrat Inayat Khan speaks about two types of knowledge. There is a knowledge that comes from the outside, from communication with people and from experience. It's a kind of wisdom, too. Then he speaks about the knowledge that has its origin in the "storehouse of all knowledge," which is the soul—and which you are born with. It is your participation in the thinking of humanity. All of the knowledge that we have about things in the world refers to this kind of superior knowledge that most of us are unaware of. For example, you're able to recognize that a tree is a tree because somewhere in your soul there is the image of a tree; seeing the tree only reminds you of something you already know. Murshid spoke about this knowledge of the soul that is inborn and is the only thing that gives us an insight into the meaning of life, and he used this in helping people who had problems. People used to flock from all parts of the world to his summer school, with their quandaries and their pangs in their hearts and their soul-searchings. You could see that they were weighed down by their problems or all caught up in their problems. But in a few days, they began to lighten up a little bit; you would see them smile a little more; and then finally they would open up just like a flower in the sun, and they would be full of joy.

People were totally transformed by the presence of Murshid, as if by the sun of his being. And did he try to unravel their problems or discuss them like a psychologist and try to find a solution? No; it wouldn't have worked. It doesn't work today, and it wouldn't have worked then, because it's not a question of the mind. Murshid gave a clue to what he was doing when he said that he is working on higher planes. The psychologist is working on the material plane, but Murshid was actually working on the higher planes. In his morning meditations he was meditating on those people—they didn't even have to be present—and working on their souls instead of their minds. Then, of course, it affected them at the level of the mind by working at that very high level—although, of course, it could only affect them if they could be carried into the ecstasy of his being. It's a kind of attunement; what he was doing was allowing us to share in his ecstasy in discovering the presence of the Beloved.

This is the greatest force that moves people in the world— the power of ecstasy. We all know that there are some moments when we are low-key, when there is a lack of magnetism of the soul. Nothing turns us on, life is very drab and dull and doesn't seem to make sense. We can't be interested in anything or muster enthusiasm for anything, because the magnetism is running low. Murshid would say this is because we have either fallen out of love with the only Being one ever loves—who is God—or have never been touched by the magic of love, which is the magic that transforms a being altogether. The magic of love is that the one who is in love makes everyone else be in love. And here was Murshid, making us be in love—but also making us awaken from the illusion of love and realizing that the one we really love is God.

This sounds flat if you say it in words, and if you're really not in love and you speak about love, it's terribly boring, terribly insincere, and hypocritical; and so the Sufi would rather remain silent. He would rather play music, because when you play music you don't have to put on any kind of show. You can only play music if you are really in love. And, of course, Hazrat Inayat Khan was, from the beginning until the end, always the musician. We could say, "Once a musician, always a musician," even though he abandoned his vina, which he had to do. I can imagine what it cost to have to abandon it, because music is not just a wonderful language in which you can express things you could never express in words, it is also a way of attunement. It's a means of finding your way back into your real attunement. When you've been out of sorts and can't find your proper inner attunement, or have lost your center, then the music comes as an expression of your nostalgia for the most beautiful thing in the world.

In fact, there's a very strong need of beauty in us. It's deadly to live without beauty—it's unbearable. Beauty is much more important than food or understanding or anything in the world. It consists, of course, in discovering the deepest aspect of our being; the easiest way to put it into words is to say that it is a higher consciousness. I get more and more wary of words: we think that we've said something by saying it with the right words when in fact we've betrayed what we're saying by finding the right word. Murshid battled with this; he said, "God speaks to the prophet in His divine tongue, and the prophet interprets it in the language of man." The mystic is always looking for the language that is going to convey something that the language cannot convey. That's why music is so wonderful—because the language is right there: it comes right out of your soul, you don't have to seek for it.

I was very young when Hazrat Inayat Khan passed away—I was ten years old. I remember receiving the telegram. We couldn't believe it. It was as if our whole world had been shattered—had come to an end. We didn't think it was possible to live without him. We couldn't believe that we wouldn't see him again. It was totally unacceptable. As a matter of fact, just a few months before that I had had my one and only interview with Hazrat Inayat Khan. His time was always taken up: there were always *mureeds*. He generally slept just about four hours a night, and when he wasn't giving interviews or talks he was meditating. I used sometimes to knock on the door of the Oriental Room, but he would be meditating, so I didn't want to disturb him. I remember that on occasion I took it upon myself to walk into the room and sit in a little corner somewhere and be very quiet and watch him repeat the *dhikr* or a *wazifa*. It is almost impossible to convey what I was experiencing in those moments: the whole room was absolutely filled with power. It was as if you could touch the atmosphere, it was so thick, and the whole room was filled with it. Murshid used to do his practices very internally, so that you could hardly hear the words. It was almost like a whisper: the power came from within.

This time when I knocked at the door, it was during the Universal Worship service. Everyone had left and Murshid was alone. He never came to the Universal Worship service the last year, and it occurred to me that this was my opportunity to talk to him. The night before I had dreamt about missing him at the railway station. We always used to go and say good-bye to him at the station, and when he arrived, we would go and fetch him at the station and he would give us little toys, as all fathers do. But I had dreamt that I had missed going to the station and that I would never see him again, and that I had missed the opportunity of going to the station for the last time. And in the course of the night, I screamed. Murshid was in the next room; he heard me scream and said, "Bhaijan," which means "dear brother" and was what he called me, "it's all right." And as I knocked at the door of the Oriental Room, I remembered the dream.

Hazrat Inayat Khan was looking out the window. My mother was taking the three other children to the Universal Worship, and he was watching her and the others going up to the hall. He was very silent and pensive. I said, "Abba, why do you not go to the Universal Worship?" And he said, "It is time for the *mureeds* to look after themselves." My dream came back to me, and I said, "But they could never look after themselves." There was a long moment of silence, and then he said, "Yes, there are going to be very difficult times. People are going to fight against each other. All of the evil in the hearts of people will come up again." When I look at this now, in perspective, I realize that it is only the power of the master that is able to hold back the aggressiveness and the evil in the hearts of men; and when I look at the problems in the world today, I realize that the world is delivered unto itself without the power of controlling those forces. The result is conflict.

We have every reason to be anxious, to be worried, to be concerned about conditions in the world, because it is absolutely inevitable that unless there is a spiritual power to hold people, just as the animal trainer controls the wild animals in the circus—unless there is a master who is able to control all these forces, they will attack each other. All the forces of hatred and jealousy and all the ugly things that are in the hearts of people will come forth. And the only person who can master the forces of evil is someone who has mastered himself.

Murshid was the master of himself, and he taught the way of the master. He said that if your horse does not obey you it is because your fingers do not obey you. If you control yourself, you can control situations. What does he mean by this control? Is it just sitting in yoga or just controlling your mind? No; he means that if you can overcome the forces of hatred in yourself, then you can hold people at bay in their hatred for one another. The forces of hatred will be there, but somehow, because you are able to overcome any hatred in yourself, your influence will hold people, up to a point. Of course, sometimes a lion will attack his trainer; but the trainer will always watch the lions and never let them out of his sight, even for one moment. Murshid was dealing with people who were not any worse or any better than anyone else. You mustn't think that because you are initiated into the Sufi Order you are better than anyone else. It is that kind of thinking that is the highest form of hypocrisy, and it does lead towards conflicts. Any sense of personal status will immediately lead towards conflict; in fact, most conflicts are just about the status of a person—that's what people are fighting for. You can see that around you in politics, as a question of losing face. People say, "I can't lose face because I represent a big nation," but there's another big nation that can't lose face either, so we start blowing each other up and blowing up the whole planet. This is why spiritual power is of greater importance in our time than ever before in the history of the world.

Murshid made us conscious of the controlling action of what he called "the spiritual government of the world." Most people had no idea about it; most people came to him with their little problems. But what he was teaching them was that there is a real government behind the world—that the hand of God manifests as a kind of guidance that is served by beings who represent this government. Murshid had a strong social sense; most people don't realize how well informed he was about the problems of his time. He was, in fact, an answer to the problems of his time, because he wasn't just teaching meditation. He wasn't just teaching people how to control their brainwaves or sit still for hours and hours contemplating their bellybuttons; he was making us conscious of meditation as part of life. That is one of the most vital aspects of his teachings: meditation in action. He teaches you to use the circumstances in your life as an opportunity to develop insight. For example, what are the qualities that you are supposed to develop in yourself in order to meet your problems? Instead of closing yourself off in an ivory tower of preconceived ideas, which is the place a lot of people meditate in, you consider life to be the live theme of meditation. It's surprising, in fact, how seldom Murshid even used the word "meditation." Often he used the word "realization" instead of "meditation," because the whole of life was a meditation.

We might call this the social aspect of meditation: instead of closing yourself up in your little personal ivory tower, you come out and experience and enter into the mind of God in His consciousness of what's happening in the world. You can see what a cosmic form of meditation that is, as opposed to closing yourself up in a kind of samadhi.

To return to my interview with Murshid, there he was looking at the people going up to the hall in a state of supreme ecstasy and saying to me, "Yes, there will be very difficult times." He knew that the difficult times come when the forces of ego are unleashed and there is no one to master them. When a teacher dies, be he a guru or a *murshid,* the disciples begin to grow in their egos because generally there is no one who has the status to master these forces. Murshid was looking at me and seeing the whole future before him, and he could see how hard it was going to be. He said, "If it was just giving teaching, it would not have been that difficult." All of a sudden, I could feel, in a way, the heartbreak. "If I had stayed in the East," he said, "I would have been sitting under a tree next to the Ganges, and people would have come and bowed their heads in the dust and I could have given them blessings." This was the tradition in which he was brought up. There would have been thousands and thousands of people coming, as they do in India today; the teacher doesn't give teachings, people come to receive his *darshan.* They come for miles, because they feel that they could never reach his realization, but some of his glory can be reflected upon them and help them to live.

I'm sure that Murshid suffered very much by the lack of finesse of some of the people he encountered. He has said that people would have liked him to say things like a hammer. People used to think, "Well, why can't you just say it? Why do you have to be so subtle about it?" When, of course, there is no language to say the real thing. Whatever you can say with language is a total distortion, and certainly a limitation of the truth that you should convey. In the one brief moment when I met him, Murshid was looking back into the past and forward into the future, and there was great sadness in his eyes. I was absolutely flabbergasted by the implications of what he was saying. "If it had been only to teach, it wouldn't have been a problem," he said. "But the problems came when dealing with the administration." That's where the strife comes in. People say, "I am a leader, and that person doesn't respect me as a leader," and so forth. When the ego is involved, that's where the problems arise. And the fact was that the teaching was not a theory: the teaching has to do with just that—with real life.

People used to come to Murshid and say, "Could you teach me meditation?" And he would say, "There's work to be done." The teaching was about dealing with real problems, instead of the very artificial kind of spirituality we see very often, which is just in the mind and doesn't correspond to reality. When a person like that is confronted with a problem, all the ignorance and hatred come up again, because they haven't been dealt with. The only way to deal with these things is to bring meditation into everyday life.

How did Murshid do this? As I said before, he was working on the higher planes. People used to come for an interview, just as I did, knocking at the door. Of course, they had an appointment, and sometimes they would have waited for two or three years before they could have perhaps five minutes to speak with Hazrat Inayat Khan. They would have prepared their whole list of questions, and they would be very worried about how they could approach this being. In the East, if you go to visit most of the gurus, you have to prostrate yourself at their feet; they sit on a throne, and you dare not even address a question to them. You certainly would not be able to discuss things in any way or have any exchange; there would just be that feeling of distance and of separation—a sort of socially accepted difference people establish in human beings that doesn't correspond to reality.

So all of a sudden the door of the Oriental Room would open and Hazrat Inayat Khan would be standing there with both hands outstretched and saying, "Come in!" The person wouldn't be able to believe that he was being welcomed by this great master just like a friend. And Murshid would say, "Come and sit next to me." In India, the disciple is supposed to sit on the floor, and the teacher sits up on his throne. But Murshid would sit on the divan and speak like an old friend. Some people were really embarrassed, because they hadn't expected that, and they didn't know how to deal with this being who was so great and who was like a friend. In their embarrassment, they didn't know what to say, so sometimes he would say, "It's all right, we don't have to speak. We'll just sit here, and it's just nice to see you and just enjoy. Let's sit here peacefully and enjoy." And then there would be a knock at the door before the person had time to think, and he would be ushered away. Then he might think to himself, "Good God, I didn't ask the questions I had in mind. My one opportunity, and it's gone! And I'll probably never be able to have an interview with Murshid again!" But when people got back home, it occurred to them that their question had been answered. They didn't have to ask it, because what Murshid had done was to attune their consciousness to such a pitch that they were able to see it themselves.

That's the method Murshid was using. He never told people what to do, but he brought his disciples to a point where they were able to see the answer themselves. When you see something you hadn't seen that way before, there's a moment of jubilation. A little child at a puzzle who suddenly sees how it fits together has that moment of joy; you can imagine what it means, then, to see, suddenly, the whole meaningfulness of your life. That's what Murshid was doing: making people see the purpose of their lives; and this is what we need most in life, to have something to live for. Our problems are not what we think they are—the material problems such as whether we should take this job, or move to Chicago, or whatever. Having to decide this or that is not where the problems are. The real problems are very, very deep; the real problems are in our need for fulfillment, our desperate need to make sense of life and to have the strength to live.

This is what Murshid was giving people: a sense of a purpose that was far beyond their own personal purpose. We know that life is only worthwhile if one is pursuing a purpose that is greater than one's own personal purpose—and that was the meaning of the Message. He was revealing something to us that is so great that our personal problems seem to fall into oblivion. It was just so wonderful to lend all our energy to fulfilling this great purpose, the only thing that really makes sense of life. There are words to say it, of course—there are always words to describe something that can't be said in words —and he said, "Of course, it is serving the Message in our time."

What greater purpose could there be than to work for the well-being of humanity? And it doesn't mean propagating ideas; when people ask, "What is the Message?", you're most embarrassed if you try to describe the Message in words. It's impossible. You can use metaphors, and of course that's what Murshid did. He would say, "It's like a rain that falls on a barren land," or "It's like sunshine," or "It's a message of hope," or "It's an answer to the cry of humanity." He said, "My deep sigh rises above as a cry of the earth," which was like the consciousness of the whole of humanity—a kind of sigh, a longing for guidance, as if to say, "Where now? What's the next step?" That is the need for guidance. Murshid said that the purpose is like the horizon, so the further you advance, the further it recedes; at no time can you say, "This is the purpose." But there are moments when the clouds have been swept away from the horizon and you can see the mountains in the distance you hadn't seen before, and the perspective is wide; you have a feeling that here is great fulfillment. But as you advance towards those mountains, you find that there are still others behind them.

So Murshid said that every soul is born with a purpose, and that purpose is ignited as one goes along. He even says that you must think of God not as the Creator who at one time decided upon the whole fate of humanity, but as the Artist who keeps on improving His work of art—and you are both the Artist and the work of art. You are the very Being who is making your life, and you are part of His life, because it is all one Being. That was the Message of Hazrat Inayat Khan.

We are gathered together here in the land he came from—where his body came from, and where his body longed to be buried—at that very spot. There is a kind of longing of the earth to return to the earth. When he returned to India in 1926, he found it very changed. You can imagine how he would feel now. He said, "It is not the India that I knew." The India he had known was a land of idealists, a land of people who were totally dedicated to the spiritual life and who had a great sense of nobility and dignity and truth. He found that the morals of people had degraded; people were lying and cheating and fighting each other; and he was very disappointed. All those things he had valued were still there, but there was less of them.

There were some holy men he met, because it is a law of nature that when a holy man is walking somewhere, another holy man comes and meets him. He met what remained of the whole heritage of India. Then he knew that his days were numbered, and he spent many nights meditating at the *dargah* of Hazrat Mu'in ad-din Chishti in Ajmer, sitting at the very *dargah* where he had sat so many years ago and where he had been given his briefing to bring the message of Sufism to the West. When he came back to Delhi, he was not feeling very well—in fact, he had pneumonia. He met a great *pir,* Hasan Nizami, who invited him to be his guest for supper. Murshid said of course he would come for supper; and then he said, "One day I shall come to stay." The *pir* knew that he meant he would be buried here one day. So when Pir Nizami heard that Hazrat Inayat Khan's body had passed away, he made arrangements for a piece of land to be obtained at the place dearest to Murshid: Nizamuddin.

Nizamuddin is a place of saints. If you walk around in it, you'll find that it's full of the ruins of very beautiful buildings. They may look very dilapidated now, but if you look behind the appearance of things, you'll realize that it is a place of wonders. The expression of the spirituality of the Sufis is everywhere you look; the remainder of the *hal*—the state of ecstasy of the Sufis—is embodied in the very stone. Murshid felt the call for his body to be buried in these surroundings, and we can feel at his *dargah* the atmosphere of Hazrat Inayat Khan everywhere in the earth, still vibrating. The ancient Hindu tradition is that the body is just the body—just a • formation. But according to the Sufis, the body is imprinted with the nature of the soul, and therefore it is not just the body. It carries great magnetism, and that magnetism can be felt here. That's why you have come here: to be in contact with the traces of the traceless here in the land of India.